Disclaimer

You care about your health and wellbeing. You understand the importance of nourishing yourself from the inside.

And you know what? I care about your health and happiness too.

That's why I've written this Keto Diet Instant Pot Cookbook.

I don't want you to waste time in the kitchen, I don't want to overwhelm you with unnecessary details that will just get you confused. But I DO want to give you delicious, mouth-watering, utterly yummy food that you will love.

Having said that, I'm not a medical professional and I'm not qualified to give you medical advice. For that reason, please consult a medical professional before following this diet, especially if you have a pre-existing health problem. By following this diet, you agree to do so at your own risk and assume all associated risk involved.

The information in this book (including nutritional content) is for informational purposes only and is not intended to be construed as medical advice nor should it replace the guidance of a qualified instructor who can guide you personally and tailor a Ketogenic diet program to your specific requirements.

Bear in mind that there are no 'typical' results from the information provided - as individuals differ, the results will differ.

No responsibility is taken for any loss or damage related directly or indirectly to the information in this book. Never disregard professional medical advice or delay in seeking it because of something you have read in this book or in any linked materials.

Table of Contents

Introduction 9

Chapter 1: Everything You Need to Know about The Ketogenic Diet 11

What is the difference between Keto and Atkins? 11

How does Keto work? 11

What will I be eating? 12

What should I expect when I switch? 12

I'm really overweight. Can I follow the Keto diet? 12

Who 'invented the Keto diet'? 12

What are the benefits of the Keto diet? 13

Chapter 2: Foods to Eat and Foods to Avoid on the Keto Diet 14

Foods to Enjoy 14

Foods to Avoid 18

Chapter 3: Beginner's Guide to the Instant Pot 22

The Benefits of Instant Pots 22

The Buttons on Your Instant Pot 23

Chapter 4: Ketogenic Instant Pot RECIPES 25

Breakfast 25

Coconut Nutmeg Porridge 25

Poblano Cheese Frittata 26

Green Onion & Ham Cups 27

Cheeseburger Casserole 28

Sous Vide Egg Bites 30

Keto Morning Meatloaf 31

Broccoli and Ham Frittata 32

Crustless Crab Quiche...33

Fast Veggie Egg Cups...34

Sausage and Veggie Egg Muffins..35

Coconut Yoghurt...36

Soup/Stew Recipes..37

Chicken Noodle Soup 37

Sausage and Kale Soup...39

Chicken Bacon Chowder...40

Pumpkin and Coconut Soup..41

Buffalo Chicken Soup..42

Chicken Enchilada Soup..43

Broccoli & Cheese Soup..45

Kimchi Beef Stew..46

Beef Curry Stew 47

Bacon Cheeseburger Soup...48

Ground Beef and Cabbage Soup..49

Beef Stew...50

Poblano Chicken Soup...51

Beef, Tomato and Cabbage Soup..52

Low Carb Zuppa Toscana Soup...53

Mexican Chicken Soup..54

Italian Sausage Soup...55

Hungarian Goulash..56

Low Carb Vegetable Soup...57

Greek Lemon Chicken Soup..58

Jalapeno Popper Soup...60

Meat Chicken...62

Garlic Chipotle Lime Chicken...62

Spaghetti Squash Chicken Alfredo 63

Creamy Salsa Chicken 65

Cool Ranch Chicken 66

Coconut Curry Chicken 67

Rosemary Chicken with Bacon & Cheese 68

Garlic and Spinach Chicken...70

Chicken with Creamy Mushroom Gravy 71

Sweet & Spicy Barbecue Chicken Wings 72

Lemon and Garlic Chicken Legs 73

Parmesan and Asiago Fried Chicken 74

Creamy Garlic Tuscan Chicken Thighs 75

Coconut Chicken 77

Belizean Stewed Chicken 78

Buffalo Chicken Cauliflower 79

Chicken Cacciatore 80

Chicken Piccata 81

Roasted Rotisserie Chicken 82

Indian Butter Chicken 83

Chicken Chili No Beans 84

Taiwanese Three Cup Chicken (San Bei Ji)...85

Jamaican Chicken Curry.. 86

Pakistani Karahi Chicken 87

Easy BBQ Chicken Wings 88

Beef 89

Keto Shepherd's Pie 89

Butter Beef 91

No Noodle Beef Lasagna..92

Balsamic Beef...93

Beef Kheema Meatloaf 94

Beef Short Ribs 95

Mexican Shredded Beef 96

Beef Chili Recipe 97

Fast Italian Meatballs 98

Italian Beef with Peppers 99

Cheese Steak Pot Roast 100

Indian Kheema Beef 101

Beef Stroganoff 102

Pork 103

Mexican Pulled Pork 103

Pork Short Ribs 104

Pork Chile Verde 105

Smothered Pork Chops 107

Korean Spicy Pork 109

Spicy Cajun Pork & Spinach Feast 110

Ginger Pork Tenderloin 111

Creamy Parmesan Garlic Pork Chops 112

Cheesy Pork with Noodles 113

Buttery Pork Chops 114

Lamb 115

Kashmiri Lamb Rogan Josh 115

Greek Lamb Gyros 116

Lamb Korma Curry 117

Leg of Lamb with Gravy 118

Seafood 119

Brazilian Fish Stew 119

Shrimp with Tomatoes and Feta 120

Chinese Style Steamed Ginger Scallion Fish 121

Easy Shrimp with Coconut Milk 122

Steamed Fish Patra Ni Maachi 123

Salmon with Orange Ginger Sauce 124

Coconut Fish Curry 125

Hearty Fish Chowder Recipe 127

Lemon-Dill Salmon & Asparagus 128

Salmon with Chili-Lime Sauce 129

Vegan/Vegetarian & Egg 130

Vegetarian Butter "Chicken" with Soy Curls 130

Korean Bibimbap 132

Korean Style Steamed Eggs 133

Eggs de Provence 134

Devilled Egg Salad 135

Saag Paneer 136

Cauliflower Mashed Potatoes 137

Side Recipes 138

Cauliflower and Cheese 138

Prosciutto Wrapped Spinach and Artichoke Chicken Bundles 139

Yakisoba Noodles 140

Low Carb Ham and Greens 141

Baked Chicken Poppers 142

Keto Brussel Sprouts 143

Final Words 144

Introduction

'My Instant Pot transformed my life.'

Or should that be, 'The Keto diet transformed my life'?

Because without both of these things I'd be completely and utterly lost.

I'd still be struggling to fasten my XXL pants.

I'd still be embarrassingly out of breath after crawling up just one flight of stairs. I'd still be hiding my body under endless tent-like clothes (usually black), trying desperately to hide the evidence of the dietary crimes I'd committed throughout my life.

I'd still be living off takeout, instant mac'n'cheese, donuts, cookies, white bread, burgers and fries and anything else that could make it onto my plate fast.

I'd still be struggling desperately with whatever new fad diet came my way, trying hard to survive on lettuce leaves and apples for the day, only to crash and binge after just a couple of hours.

The truth was, I was destined for an early grave.

The number on the scale was moving, but not in the direction I wanted it to.

I didn't know what to do. I wasn't the dieting type. I didn't like veggies much anyway. And my willpower? Well let's not talk about it...

Besides, I wasn't privileged enough to be able to buy fancy organic foods from Wholefoods- I had to work several jobs to make ends meet. I just didn't have time to hang around in the kitchen, cooking food from scratch. And why would I, anyway, when someone else could do it all for me?

But everything changed when I discovered the Keto diet and invested in an Instant pot.

I was finally able to take control of my eating habits and start choosing healthier (and often cheaper) options, safe in the knowledge that I had enough time to nourish myself like this.

It wasn't about deprivation. It wasn't about sacrificing time. It wasn't about hating myself, then starving myself.

It was all positive and utterly delicious!

Now I'm here to help the same thing happen in your life.

Whether you're a complete beginner when it comes to the Keto diet, or you've been following it for a while, I promise that you'd get something new and useful out of this book. And whether you've never even seen an Instant Pot, or you're already a pro, you'll also find tons of inspiring recipes here that you will love.

What to expect

In the chapters that follow, I'll start by giving a quick rundown of the Keto diet, including what it's all about, its health benefits, its history, and what you can and can't eat. Then I'll do the same with the Instant Pot, and explain what it is, what it does and how to use it. I'll include an explanation of all the buttons that might be on your particular model of Instant Pot, so you can even move forward and start experimenting once you're feeling more confident.

Finally comes the best bit of all- the recipes! I've included over 100 Keto Instant Pot recipes to help you get started on this culinary adventure of a lifetime. This includes breakfasts, soups and stews, side dishes, poultry, lamb, pork, beef, seafood, fish, eggs and even some vegetarian/vegan recipes at the end.

I've kept the ingredients at a minimum wherever possible, and really cut back on the instructions so you can quickly read exactly what you need to do as you cook.

As you'd expect, the majority of the recipes are extremely low carb to fit with the rules of the Ketogenic diet. However, there are times where I'll include a recipe which is slightly higher in carbs, usually around 8-10g per portion. These are absolutely fine to eat on most versions of the Keto diet, provided you keep a careful eye on the food you eat for the rest of that day.

So, with all of that out of the way, will you join me as I guide you through 100 mouth-watering recipes for the Ketogenic diet and inspire you to get cooking! *Enjoy!*

Chapter 1: Everything You Need to Know about The Ketogenic Diet

The Ketogenic Diet is the perfect way to keep eating those delicious, satisfying and nourishing foods you LOVE without ever having to worry about your weight.

You won't have to nibble lettuce leaves or fight hunger pangs with this diet. You won't need to force yourself to eat foods that you detest just because you want to drop a pound or two. We're all about pleasure in this game!

You're probably wondering how this can be possible? After all, aren't ALL diets about depriving yourself and sweating it out at the gym?

The answer is no. Not when you eat the low carb Keto way.

What is the difference between Keto and Atkins?

The Keto is very low carb, much lower than the Atkins diet because it aims to get your body into a state of Ketosis (or at least, as close as possible) to help you burn fat fast. Whilst the Atkins diet is very protein heavy, the Keto diet places a greater emphasis on healthy fats.

How does Keto work?

Carbs and sugars are the main source of fuel for your body and your brain. But eaten in excess, they can also cause you to gain weight, and store it in the places you like the least. Around your stomach, your hips, on your butt and on your upper arms. (Hello flabby arms!!)

But it doesn't have to be this way.

By reducing your carb intake, and instead filling up on healthy fats and protein, your body will switch to burning fat as its main source of fuel.

When you burn fat instead of carbs, guess when it comes from? Not just the food you're eating, but right from those trouble spot on your body. This means you can literally go to bed one night and wake up slimmer. It's awesome when you witness this happening with your own eyes, trust me!

What will I be eating?

On a Keto diet, you'll be eating a diet of around 70-80% fat, 25% protein and 5% carbs. This will include a variety of colorful, delicious, mouth-watering, inspiring foods from all food groups. (You can read more about what you can and can't eat in a moment).

What should I expect when I switch?

Sometimes when you start the Keto diet and your body switches its main energy source from carbs to fats, you might experience a couple of 'detox' symptoms. Don't worry, this stage usually doesn't last for long and can be easily managed by drinking plenty of water and getting plenty of rest.

Once your body is solely using fats as fuels, you are in a phase known as Ketosis.

Bear in mind that not everyone following a Keto diet necessarily needs to enter a state of Ketosis (although purists might disagree.) In fact, many doctors now recommend that you instead follow a very low carb diet with the only source of carbs coming from very small amounts of vegetables, rather than a full Ketogenic diet. Having said that, the choice is yours!

I'm really overweight. Can I follow the Keto diet?

Yep- almost everyone can safely follow the Ketogenic diet. This includes most adults and some children too (under the supervision of a doctor.) However, please do consider seeking medical advice before you switch to the Keto diet, especially if you are diabetic, taking insulin, you have high blood pressure, or you're pregnant or breastfeeding.

Who 'invented the Keto diet'?

The Keto diet was invented by doctors at the Mayo clinic as a way of controlling certain types of epilepsy in children. As more people noticed its benefits for overall heath and weight control, it grew in popularity to become the well-known diet that it is today.

What are the benefits of the Keto diet?

We've touched on this above, but I think it's worth discussing more of the benefits of the Keto diet, as they are so far-reaching, exciting and life-changing.

- You'll lose weight effortlessly- The Keto diet helps weight drop off without depriving yourself of the foods you love.

- Your brain will get a boost- All that healthy fat boosts brain function and will help you learn faster and become more productive than ever before. Awesome!

- Your stamina will grow- Fat is a much more efficient fuel source than carbs and you have a generous store of it in your body (unlike carbs which you need to keep topping up.)

- Your hormones will balance- Carbs and sugars interfere with the regulation of hormones around our bodies. Cut them out and your hormones will rebalance easily.

- You'll feel less hungry- Keto is just about eating food you love until you feel satisfied.

- Your heart will get healthier- Keto reduces levels of bad cholesterol in your blood and raises the levels of that good stuff. Awesome.

- Your epilepsy symptoms might improve- Keto was invented for you!

- Your migraines could reduce- The Keto diet appears to reduce the levels of glutamate in the brain which has been linked to migraine attacks. Read more about this here.

- You'll protect yourself against cancer- Carbs and sugar feed cancerous cells so reducing your intake will help them to die.

As you can see, the Keto diet is the perfect solution for the modern, active, healthy and more of all, slim lifestyle.

However, there's a huge part of the diet that we haven't yet touched on, and that's the small matter of what you can actually eat on this diet. Turn to the next chapter where I will explain all...

Chapter 2: Foods to Eat and Foods to Avoid on the Keto Diet

If you're a Keto diet newbie, your head might be spinning a bit at this point as you try to take everything in. But don't worry- this is completely normal when you get started. Soon you'll reach for your favorite foods without needing to think too much about whether it's Keto-friendly or not.

To help you get started, or refresh your memory, I'm about the share a comprehensive list of which foods you should be enjoying as part of your healthy Ketogenic diet, and which foods you should be avoiding.

Don't let it overwhelm you- just remember that healthy fats, meat, fish, poultry and seafood are fine. Certain veggies are fine. High-carb foods are best avoided.

Foods to Enjoy

Meat, Poultry, Fish and Seafood

You can eat any of these you fancy. For maximum health benefits, try to choose organic and grass-fed as much as possible and don't think you need to trim away the fat- you don't. Just make sure you avoided breaded fish as it contains breadcrumbs.

Enjoy it all!

- Beef
- Pork
- Lamb
- Game
- Chicken
- Turkey
- Organ meats
- Salmon
- Mackerel

- Sardines
- Herring
- Cod

Eggs

Eggs are fabulous on the Keto diet as they're a great source of protein and B-complex vitamins, and they taste great. Eat them however you like- boiled, scrambled, fried, poached, or even cooked into 'breads'.

Dairy Products

Great news- all dairy products are on the menu with the Keto diet. And I'm not talking about those low-fat, zero-flavor fake dairy products either. I'm talking about full fat, awesome taste, and hugely satisfying regular dairy.

Include as much butter, cream, sour cream, hard and soft cheeses and Greek or Turkish yoghurt as you like. Whilst you absolutely can drink regular, full-fat cow's milk, I'd advise you don't overdo it. Milk does contain quite significant quantities of carbs (11.03g for just 1 cup/235ml) so be careful!

Fats, Oils and Sauces

Unlike many slimming diets, the Keto diet allows you to include as much healthy fat as you desire. This includes:

- Butter
- Cream
- Coconut oil
- Olive oil
- Ghee
- Chicken fat
- Avocados
- Mayonnaise
- High-fat sauces

Please do avoid those unhealthy fats such as trans fats and polyunsaturated vegetable fats as much as possible. Whilst they *are* allowed on the Keto diet, they're harmful to your health, highly processed and best avoided.

Vegetables

Most vegetables are quite high in carb and are best avoided (more on this in a moment). However, there are some which are surprisingly low-carb and a great source of vitamins, minerals and antioxidants, making them a great addition to your Keto diet. Again, don't go crazy with these- even minimal carbs add up after a while!

Great choices include:

- Green leafy veggies like kale, collards, Bok choy & spinach
- Cauliflower
- Broccoli
- Cabbage
- Brussels sprouts
- Asparagus
- Zucchini
- Eggplant
- Olives
- Mushrooms
- Cucumber
- Lettuce
- Avocado
- Onions
- Garlic

Herbs and Spices

Great news if you're a big fan of flavor- you can add any kind of herb or spice to your food you desire when you're following a Keto diet and lifestyle. Whether you love to pick fresh herbs straight from your garden or you prefer an Indian-style blend of warming spices like cumin, coriander and turmeric, you'll LOVE what the Keto diet can offer.

If you buy your spices from the store, please double-check the label to ensure that it's 100% sugar-free and gluten-free. You'd be surprised how many brands add these two ingredients to their products.

Sauces and Condiments

You will need to avoid certain sauces and condiments on the Keto diet as many of them are high-carb. Having said that, there are still plenty of extras you can add to your food to boost the flavor. Check the list above of herbs and spices to remind you.

If you're looking for more, you can also add the following to your food:

- Soy Sauce
- Lemon and lime juice
- Sriracha Sauce
- Homemade mayo
- Dijon mustard
- Wholegrain mustard (but check the label)
- Hot sauces (but check the label)
- Salad dressings (homemade only)

Sweeteners

You can split Keto-fans into two groups- those who believe in using sweeteners in their foods and those who don't. Whichever camp you fall into, you might find it useful to know which of them you can use if the mood takes you to eat something which tastes sweet.

- Erythritol
- Stevia
- Splenda
- Brand-name sugar replacements

Alcoholic and Non-Alcoholic Drinks

The best choices for drinks on the Keto diet are those simple options which are also thirst-quenching and taste great.

My favorites are tea, coffee and water. If you're drinking someplace like Starbucks, be sure to avoid those added extras like syrups, sugars and so on. By all means, add as much milk or cream as you like, or go one step further and do it Bulletproof Coffee-style.

Alcohol is also on the menu, provided you don't go crazy with it, and don't choose sweet cocktails or high-sugar lagers.

Safer options include champagne, red or white wine, whiskey, tequila, vodka, soda Dry Martini and brandy. A glass or two shouldn't hurt!

Snacks

Snacks aren't a food group, but they are very much worth mentioning here as they help bridge the gap between meals and, let's be honest, make life worth living!

Healthy ideas include:

- Celery with nut butter
- Nuts and seeds (not cashew nuts)
- Hard-boiled eggs
- Bacon rashers
- Ham Roll-Ups (filled with avocado and cucumber or scrambled eggs)
- Sliced cucumber, avocado and celery
- Sauerkraut and Kimchi
- Pork rinds and crackling
- Fat bombs

Foods to Avoid

Now we've talked about the best bit (the foods you can keep enjoying), let's have a quick look at what you need to avoid on the Ketogenic diet. Don't worry- it's not as bad as you might think!

Sugar

Sugar is the most important thing to avoid on the Keto diet because sugars and carbs are essentially the same thing.

The easiest way to avoid sugar is to stop eating processed foods and start cooking from scratch more often. Most manufacturers add huge quantities of sugar to their foods (even the savory ones), so you'll often be surprised to discover what really contains sugar when you check.

Next, stop adding sugar to your hot drinks. Then check the following list:

- Soft drinks
- Fruit yoghurts
- Premade cereal bars
- Smoothies
- Candy
- Juice
- Sports drinks
- Chocolate
- Cake

- Buns
- Pastries
- Ice cream
- Donuts
- Cookies
- Breakfast cereals

Carbs and grains

Avoid all of these without question- they're high carb!

- Wheat
- Barley
- Oats
- Rice
- Rye
- Corn
- Quinoa
- Millet
- Sorghum
- Bulgur
- Amaranth
- Sprouted grains
- Buckwheat

This includes foods made from these ingredients, (wholegrain, wholemeal, brown, white and corn) which include:

- Bread
- Pasta
- Rice
- Potatoes
- French fries
- Potato chips
- Porridge
- Oats
- Muesli

Beans & Lentils

Bad news for vegetarians and vegans- beans and lentils are largely off the menu if you're following the Keto diet faithfully. You'll need to avoid: ☐

- Red, green, brown and black lentils
- Red Kidney beans
- Black-Eye beans
- Chickpeas
- Black beans
- Green peas
- Lima beans
- Pinto beans
- White beans
- Fava beans

What about margarine, beer and fruit?

I'm always getting asked about these three confusing foods; whether they're suitable for the Keto diet or whether they're perfectly fine. Therefore, I'd like to take a few moments to talk about each of these foods.

- **Margarine:** It's Keto-friendly, BUT not advised. There's nothing in margarine that says you have to avoid it on a Keto diet. Having said that, if you care about your health, this might not be something you really want to be putting into your body. It's full of chemical, unhealthy fats and other worrying additives. If you want to spread something on your bread or use something for cooking, stick with butter instead.
- **Alcohol:** I've mentioned in the early section about the alcoholic drinks you can continue to consume. Having said that, alcohol does contain carbs to varying degrees, so it's best to avoid them all.
- **Fruit:** Fruit is incredibly high in carbs, so you'll need to avoid it on a Keto diet. This includes fruit juice, dried fruit and smoothies too. You can occasionally eat a handful of berries if you're desperate, but it's best avoided as much as possible.
- **Unhealthy fat:** Yes, I know I said this bit would be all about margarine, alcohol and fruit, but it's important that I mention a few things about fats. Namely, that they aren't all built the same. Some fats are great for your health, and others spell disaster. The latter are to be avoided at all costs and include soybean oil, canola oil, corn oil, grapeseed oil, peanut oil, sesame oil and sunflower oil.

That should give you all the basics you need to know about which foods to include, and which you need to avoid so you can start making the Keto diet a part of your healthy lifestyle and really reap the benefits.

But before we get onto the recipes themselves, let's talk for a moment about the Instant Pot, why it's so useful for us Keto-fans and how you can use it to best effect. Turn to the next chapter to find out more.

Chapter 3: Beginner's Guide to the Instant Pot

If you're reading a book like this, it's quite likely that you already know exactly what an Instant Pot is. You know that it's a multi-functional counter top cooker that combines everything you could ever want to create incredible, delicious meals.

For the price of just one appliance you get an electric pressure cooker, a slow cooker, a rice cooker (not that you need one of these for the Keto diet!), a steamer, a sauté pan, a yoghurt maker and even a pot to keep your food warm.

Having said that, most people use their Instant pot as an electric pressure cooker with handy extras that help them create cooked meats that flake off the bone and melt in the mouth, soft flavor-rich low-carb veggies, warming soups and stews, extra-fast fish dishes and much more.

The Benefits of Instant Pots

Instant Pots are simply brilliant! Here are just a few of their benefits:

#1: They're fast

When you use an Instant Pot, you'll slash your cooking times down to a fraction of the time (the manufacturers say around 70%!!). This comes in extremely handy when you've got a demanding family to feed, a busy life and, quite frankly, plenty of things you'd rather do than standing in the kitchen.

#2: They will save you money

Instant pots use less energy than regular cooking methods, and they allow you to buy cheaper cuts of meat and save tons of money on your regular grocery bill. Also, none of the cooking water can evaporate during cooking so even the cheapest steak will taste soft, succulent and delicious.

#3: They will nourish you more

No, I don't just mean you'll be more nourished when you follow a Keto diet. Using an Instant Pot will do it! That's because it helps lock the vitamins and minerals in your food, so you get more 'bang for your buck'.

#4: You won't need as many kitchen appliances

I'm a bit of a minimalist, so any way I can save space in the kitchen is perfect. Because the Instant pot takes the place of all those appliances, a cleaner, tidier kitchen will be yours!

#5: They won't explode!

Regular pressure cookers used to scare me. Really! I always worried that they'd explode and I'd be left with a very crazy mess afterwards. No so with the Instant Pot. It features safety-regulating features which help monitor the temperature and pressure, so we can all stay safer. Having said that, please be careful. It's still steam, after all!

The Buttons on Your Instant Pot

When you've just got your hands on an Instant Pot, working out what to do with all those buttons can be quite overwhelming. I remember just what is was like. To keep things nice and easy for you, I've primarily given cooking instructions in this book using the format.

[low/high pressure] + [manual] + [cooking time]

Having said that, Instant Pots have plenty of features which you can really make the most of as you get more familiar with how to cook amazing food with your Instant Pot. Here's a quick guide to the buttons on your Instant Pot to help you explore more...

The Basics

- **Sauté** - Use this to sauté onions, garlic, vegetables and brown meat, or simmer on a lower heat.
- **Keep warm/cancel** - Press this to stop cooking or to keep your food warm.
- **Manual/pressure cook** - This is the setting I refer to throughout the recipe section.
- **Slow cooker** - This gives a default 4-hour cooking time.
- **Pressure** - This button allows you to switch between high and low pressure
- **Yoghurt** - For making...yoghurt!
- **Timer** - You can delay the start of cooking by using this setting.

Presets

- **Soup** - High pressure for 30 minutes.
- **Meat/stew** - High pressure for 35 minutes.

- **Bean/chili** - High pressure for 30 minutes.
- **Poultry** - High pressure for 15 minutes.
- **Rice** - Cooks rice automatically.
- **Multigrain** - High pressure for 40 minutes.
- **Porridge** - High pressure for 20 minutes
- **Steam** - High pressure for 10 minutes.
- **Cake** - For cooking cakes. Refer to manufacturers guide for times and settings.
- **Egg** - Cooks your eggs hard or soft boiled.
- **Sterilize** - Clean your utensils and jars with this setting.

Note that not all brands or models will have these settings.

So, if you're ready, turn the page and let me share with you 100 deliciously nourishing, extremely easy, globally-inspired Keto Instant Pot recipes that I've been working so hard on these past few months.

Chapter 4: Ketogenic Instant Pot RECIPES

Breakfast

Coconut Nutmeg Porridge

If you still crave your favorite bowl of oatmeal, then you'll LOVE this brilliant coconut version. It's hot, it's as sweet as your heart desires and it will keep you full 'til lunchtime.

Cooks: 15 mins
Serves: 6
Net carbs: 5g
Fat: 25g
Protein: 3g

Ingredients:

- 1 cup (100g) unsweetened dried coconut
- 2 cups (470ml) coconut milk
- 2 2/3 cups (730ml) water
- ¼ cup (32g) coconut flour
- ¼ cup (20g) psyllium husks
- 1 tsp. vanilla extract
- ½ tsp. cinnamon
- ¼ tsp. nutmeg
- 30 drops stevia liquid
- 20 drops monk fruit liquid

Method:

1. Preheat your Instant Pot to sauté and toast the coconut until golden.
2. Add the coconut milk and stir through.
3. Cover and set on high pressure, with timer set to zero.
4. Do a quick pressure release, open and stir in the remaining ingredients.
5. Serve and enjoy.

Poblano Cheese Frittata

There's nothing like tucking into a generous portion of cheesy, spicy frittata on a sunny morning. Trust me! It will transport you all the way to Mexico and you'll still make it back in time for work!

Cooks: 40 mins
Serves: 4
Net carbs: 5g
Fat: 10g
Protein: 14g

Ingredients:
- 4 free-range eggs
- 1 cup (235ml) half and half
- 10 oz. (280g) diced canned green chilis
- ½ - 1 tsp. salt
- ½ tsp. ground cumin
- 1 cup (125g) Mexican blend shredded cheese divided
- 4 Tbsp. chopped cilantro
- 2 cups (470ml) water

Method:
1. Take a large bowl and combine half and half, chilis, salt, cumin and half the shredded cheese.
2. Grease a pan (that will fit into your Instant Pot), pour the egg mixture inside and cover with foil.
3. Place the water into the bottom of your Instant pot, place the trivet in the bottom then place pan inside.
4. Cover and cook on high for 20 minutes.
5. Do a natural pressure release for 10 minutes then do a manual release.
6. Add the remaining cheese and pop under a broiler until the cheese has browned.
7. Serve and enjoy!

Green Onion & Ham Cups

There are days when you don't want to hang around cooking- you just want to grab and go. That's when you need one (or several!) of these. Make a big batch on the weekend and you'll have enough Keto-friendly breakfasts to last the week. Awesome!

Cooks: 15 mins

Serves: 12

Net carbs: 2 g

Fat: 2g

Protein: 9g

Ingredients:

- 4 oz. (85g) deli ham, sliced
- 2 2/3 oz. (75g) frozen hash browns
- 2 tsp. butter
- 1/3 cups (40g) Cheddar cheese, shredded
- 2 free-range eggs
- 2 tsp. milk
- 1/8 tsp. salt
- 1/8 tsp. black pepper
- 2 Tbsp. sliced green onion (Scallion)
- 1 cup (235ml) water

Method:

1. Grab some silicone muffin cups and line with the ham.
2. Take a bowl, place the hash browns and butter inside, and microwave for two minutes.
3. Place hash browns on top of ham.
4. Combine eggs, milk and seasoning in a bowl and divide between the muffin cups.
5. Top with the cheese and sprinkle with onions.
6. Place the water into the bottom of your Instant pot and add the trivet.
7. Pop the muffin cases into the Instant pot, on the trivet, cover and cook on high for 5 minutes.
8. Do a natural pressure release for ten minutes.
9. Remove, serve and enjoy!

Cheeseburger Casserole

Who ever heard of having cheeseburgers for breakfast?? Yes, my inner teenager whoops too!! But these ones have been given a healthy, Keto makeover, that keeps the flavor on max whilst dialing down the carbs. Of course, you can remove the sauces and replace with chili sauce if you prefer.

Cooks: 1 hour
Serves: 6
Net carbs: 5g
Fat: 43g
Protein: 43g

Ingredients:
- ½ lb. (112g) bacon, cooked
- 1 Tbsp. oil
- 1 lb. (225g) ground beef
- ½ sweet onion
- 1 clove garlic
- 4 Tbsp. cream cheese
- 2 Tbsp. reduced sugar ketchup
- 1 Tbsp. yellow mustard
- 1 Tbsp. low-sugar Worcestershire sauce
- 1 tsp. seasoned salt
- 4 large free-range eggs
- ¼ cup (60ml) heavy cream
- 1 tsp. ground pepper
- 1 tsp. hot sauce
- 8 oz. (225g) grated Cheddar cheese
- 1 tsp. fresh dill

Method:
1. Open up your Instant pot, turn onto sauté and add the oil. Throw in the ground beef and cook until brown.
2. Drain away the excess fat then add the onion and garlic. Cook for 5 minutes.
3. Add the remaining ingredients except the bacon, eggs, cream, pepper and hot sauce. Stir well to combine.
4. Turn off the heat and press into the bottom of the pan and top with the bacon.

28

5. Whisk the eggs together in a bowl, add the cream, pepper and hot sauce then pour over the bacon.
6. Sprinkle the cheese over the top, then cover.
7. Cook on manual high pressure for 30 minutes.
8. Do a natural pressure release for 10 minutes then a quick pressure release.
9. Serve and enjoy!

Sous Vide Egg Bites

Starbucks sell these awesome egg bites which are perfectly delicious, satisfying little nibbles that pack in the taste and keep the health benefits on max. But save your dollars and make these at home instead. Yum!

Cooks: 30
Serves: 4
Net carbs: 4g
Fat: 22g
Protein: 19g

Ingredients:

- 4 free-range eggs
- 4 bacon strips, cooked
- 1 ½ cups (185g) shredded cheese
- ½ cup (110g) cottage cheese
- ¼ cup (60ml) heavy cream
- ½ tsp. salt

Method:

1. Start by grabbing four mason jars. Crumble the bacon into the bottom.
2. Thrown the eggs, cheese, cottage cheese, cream and salt into the blender and blend until smooth.
3. Place the water into the Instant pot and drop in the trivet.
4. Spray the jars with oil and pour the egg into the jars, cover with foil and place into the Instant pot.
5. Cover, press the 'steam' button and cook for 8 minutes.
6. Do a natural pressure release for 10 minutes then quick release.
7. Serve and enjoy!

Keto Morning Meatloaf

Sausage + cheese + eggs = breakfast heaven. And don't just take my word for it. Check out this amazing morning meatloaf and you'll be a convert too! This recipe is also perfect for those meals when you can't be bothered to cook anything more complicated, but you still want to stick to your Keto principles.

Cooks: 45 mins
Serves: 4
Net carbs: 3g
Fat: 60g
Protein: 42g

Ingredients:

- 1 Tbsp. butter or ghee
- 6 free-range eggs
- 1 lb. (450g) bulk sweet Italian sausage or breakfast sausage
- ¼ yellow onion, chopped
- 4 oz. (112g) organic cream cheese (at room temperature), divided
- 1 cup (125g) shredded cheddar cheese
- 2 Tbsp. chopped scallion

Method:

1. Open up your Instant pot and grease well with the oil.
2. Whisk the eggs together in a bowl with the sausage, onion and half the cream cheese.
3. Pour into the Instant pot, cover and cook on manual high pressure for 20 minutes.
4. Do a quick pressure release then open the lid.
5. Spread the top with the remaining cream cheese, sprinkle with scallions and pop under a preheated broiler until brown.
6. Serve and enjoy!

Broccoli and Ham Frittata

There are frittatas. Then there are FRITTATAS- the ones with added touches and extra ingredients that make an average dish into a flavor-rich, super-nourishing meal you could just keep right on eating all day. With the added broccoli and ham, this one is a winner!

Cooks: 40 mins
Serves: 4
Net carbs: 7g
Fats: 30g
Protein: 28g

Ingredients:
- 8 oz. (225g) ham cubed
- 1 cup (175g) sliced sweet peppers
- 2 cups (180g) frozen broccoli
- 4 free-range eggs
- 1 cup (235ml) half and half
- 1 cup (125g) shredded cheddar cheese
- 1 tsp. salt
- 2 tsp. ground pepper
- 2 cups (480ml) water

Method:
1. Start by greasing a pan that will fit into your Instant pot.
2. Place the peppers into the bottom, then the ham and the broccoli.
3. Grab a bowl and mix together the eggs, half and half and the seasoning, followed by the cheese.
4. Pour onto the veggies and cover with foil.
5. Pour the water into the bottom of your Instant Pot, add the trivet, and finally add the pan.
6. Cover and cook on high for 20 minutes.
7. Do a natural pressure release for 10 minutes then quick release the rest.
8. Rest for 5-10 minutes then serve and enjoy!

Crustless Crab Quiche

I've always been a massive fan of seafood, but crab was never one that captured my imagination. Until I tried this crustless quiche. It has that delicate fish taste, a gentle touch of sweetness and it is packed full of brain-friendly protein that will supercharge your day.

Cooks: 50 mins
Serves: 4
Net carbs: 18g
Fat: 25g
Protein: 22g

Ingredients:

- 4 free-range eggs
- 1 cup (235ml) half and half
- ½ tsp. salt
- 1 tsp. pepper
- 1 tsp. sweet smoked paprika
- 1 tsp. Herbes de Provence
- 1 cup (125g) shredded cheese
- 1 cup (150g) chopped green onions
- 8 oz. (225g) crab meat (real or imitation)
- 2 cups (470ml) water

Method:

1. Grab a spring-form pan that will fit into your Instant pot. Line with silver foil.
2. Beat together the eggs, cream, salt, pepper, paprika and herbs.
3. Stir through the cheese, onions and crab meat.
4. Pour the egg mixture into the pan and cover with foil.
5. Place the water into the bottom of your Instant pot, add the trivet and lower the pan into the bottom.
6. Cook on high for 40 minutes.
7. Do a natural pressure release for ten minutes, then quick release the remaining pressure.
8. Serve and enjoy!

Fast Veggie Egg Cups

What better way to start the day than with eggs? They will kickstart your metabolism, satisfy your taste buds and break your fast effortlessly. I really love the fact that you can throw any low-carb veggies (or meats or cheeses) into these egg cups as you like and create your ultimate breakfast ever. Mmm...

Cooks: 15 mins
Serves: 4
Net carbs: 1g
Fat: 9g
Protein: 9g

Ingredients:
- 4 free-range eggs
- 1 cup (150g) diced vegetables such as onions, bell peppers, mushrooms
- ½ cup (62g) shredded sharp cheddar cheese
- ¼ cup (60ml) half and half
- Salt and Pepper, to taste
- 2 Tbsp. chopped cilantro (or other herb of choice)

To serve...
- ½ cup (62g) shredded cheese of choice

Method:
1. Grab four mason jars and grease well.
2. Then take a bowl and mix together the eggs, veggies, cheese, half and half, salt and pepper and the cilantro.
3. Pour the egg mixture into the jars and lightly cover with the lid (but don't tighten).
4. Place the water into the bottom of your Instant Pot, drop in the trivet and place the mason jars inside.
5. Cover and cook for 5 minutes on high.
6. Do a quick pressure release.
7. Open up and top with the remaining cheese, then broil for a few minutes until the cheese is brown.
8. Serve and enjoy!

Sausage and Veggie Egg Muffins

These delicious muffins are like an entire meal in every bite. Packed with healthy, low carb veggies, satisfying sausage and plenty of taste, you'll LOVE starting your day with these delicious treats.

Cooks: 20 minutes
Serves: 12
Net carbs: 2g
Fat: 9g
Protein: 7g

Ingredients:

- 8 oz. (225g) pork breakfast sausage
- 1 Tbsp. extra virgin olive oil
- ½ white onion
- ¾ cup ((130g) bell peppers
- 1 ½ cups spinach (45g)
- 1 tsp. fresh oregano
- 9 free-range eggs
- ¼ cup (65ml) milk
- Salt and pepper, to taste
- 2 cups (470ml) water

Method:

1. Grab some silicon muffin pans and grease well.
2. Meanwhile, preheat a pan, add a drop of oil and cook sausage meat, breaking it up nicely.
3. Next add the onions, pepper and oregano and cook for five minutes.
4. Throw in the spinach and stir well. Remove from heat and divide between pans.
5. Whisk eggs with salt, pepper and milk and pour over the sausage mixture.
6. Pour the water into the Instant pot, add the trivet and then the muffin pans.
7. Cover and cook for cover and cook on high for 5 minutes.
8. Do a natural pressure release for ten minutes.
9. Remove, serve and enjoy!

Coconut Yoghurt

Don't be deterred by the mention of probiotics in this recipe. You can easily get hold of probiotics for yoghurt making and have a rich and creamy breakfast ready for you to enjoy! If you have trouble finding it, you can also substitute for unflavored live yoghurt and if you'd prefer, you can also use regular cream instead of the coconut cream.

Cooks: 24 hours (12 hours developing plus 12 hours resting)
Serves: 5
Net carbs: 6g
Fat: 68g
Protein: 6g

Ingredients:
- 2 caps any multi-strain probiotic
- 1 x 33.8 fl. oz. (1 liter) coconut cream

Extra equipment
- 2 sterile quart-sized (approx. 1 liter) mason jars with sterile lids

Method:
1. Start by emptying a cap of the probiotics into each jar.
2. Pour the coconut cream into the jars, then pop the cap on and shake well. Remove the lids.
3. Pop the jars (without the lids) into the Instant pot and cover.
4. Cook on the yoghurt setting for 12 hours.
5. Do a quick pressure release, remove the jars and place into the fridge for at least 12 hours. This will help the yoghurt thicken.
6. Serve and enjoy!

Soup/Stew Recipes

Chicken Noodle Soup

Everyone needs a go-to chicken noodle soup recipe for those moments when you're feeling full of cold, your immune system needs a boost and you want to keep everyone's appetites completely happy. Great for busy lifestyles and delicious, you'll want to keep making this one. Trust me! If you want to lower the carbs, eliminate the carrots.

Cooks: 30 mins
Serves: 8
Net carbs: 4.9g
Fat: 13.6g
Protein: 25.5g

Ingredients:

- 10 cups (2.5l) chicken broth
- 1 lb. (450g) cooked chicken
- 1 tablespoon fresh lemon juice or apple cider vinegar
- 14 oz. (400g) shirataki noodles
- 2 medium carrots, sliced
- 4.5 oz. (135g) cauliflower, chopped
- 1 teaspoon salt
- 4 oz. (112g) broccoli, chopped
- 2 celery stalks, sliced
- 1 small zucchini, diced
- 1 small red pepper, chopped
- 1 small bunch dark leaf kale, stems removed, chopped
- 1 cup (70g) sliced white mushrooms
- ¾ cup (75g) chopped green beans
- 2 bay leaves
- 3 whole allspice
- Giblets such as sliced heart and liver, opt.

To serve...
- 4 tablespoons freshly chopped parsley
- Black pepper, to taste

Method:

1. Start by preparing the noodles according to the instructions on the packet.
2. Pour the chicken broth into the Instant pot and set to sauté.
3. Once boiling, add the veggies, bay leaves, spices and salt. Cook for 10 minutes.
4. Turn off the instant pot and stir through the noodles, chicken and parsley.
5. Season to taste, remove the bay leaves then serve and enjoy!

Sausage and Kale Soup

This one ticks all of the macro and micronutrient boxes. Protein, vitamins, minerals and the biggest one of all, the taste factor. Wow!

Cooks: 25 mins
Serves: 6
Net carbs: 6g
Fat: 3g
Protein: 20g

Ingredients:
- 1 lb. (450g) Italian turkey sausage
- 1 Tbsp. olive oil
- ½ cup (150g) onion
- 15 oz. (425g) diced tomatoes
- 32 oz. (950ml) chicken broth
- 8 oz. (225g) kale

Method:
1. Place the oil into your Instant pot, set to sauté and brown the sausage.
2. Switch off the Instant pot and add the onions, tomatoes and broth.
3. Cover with the lid and set to manual pressure (high) for 15 minutes.
4. Meanwhile, pop the kale into a bowl with ½ cup (110ml) water and microwave for 3 minutes. Remove and drain.
5. When your Instant pot has finished, do a natural pressure release then do a quick release.
6. Stir through the kale, then serve and enjoy.

Chicken Bacon Chowder

I LOVE the taste of rich, creamy chowder, flecked with herbs and powered up with chicken and bacon. It's not identical to a regular chowder but it's the best Keto version I've ever had. It's also pretty rich, so you'll be satisfied faster.

Cooks: 30 minutes
Serves: 8
Net carbs: 5.8g
Fat: 28g
Protein: 21g

Ingredients:
- 4 cloves garlic, minced
- 1 shallot, finely chopped
- 1 small leek, cleaned, trimmed and sliced
- 2 ribs celery, diced
- 6 oz. ((170g) cremini mushrooms, sliced
- 1 medium sweet onion, thinly sliced
- 4 Tbsp. butter, divided
- 2 cups (470ml) chicken stock, divided
- 1 lb. (450g) chicken breasts
- 8 oz. (225g) cream cheese
- 1 cup (240ml) heavy cream
- 1 lb. (450g) bacon, cooked crisp and crumbled
- 1 tsp. sea salt
- 1 tsp. black pepper
- 1 tsp. garlic powder
- 1 tsp. dried thyme

Method:
1. Heat your Instant pot to sauté, add the butter and brown the chicken.
2. Next add the garlic, onions, leek, celery and mushrooms and cook for five more minutes. Remove the chicken and pop to one side.
3. Stir through the stock, cream, cream cheese, garlic powder, thyme and the salt and pepper until no lumps remain.
4. Cut the chicken into chunks and add to the Instant pot. Stir through.
5. Cover and set to the soup setting. Cook for 7 minutes.
6. Allow the pressure to release naturally for 10 minutes, then do a quick pressure release.
7. Serve and enjoy!

Pumpkin and Coconut Soup

Coming in at 10g of net carbs, this soup probably won't be on the menu every day, but as a relatively lower carb addition to your soup repertoire (that is also vegan-friendly), it's brilliant. Rich, creamy and simple, it's perfect for those colder days.

Cooks: 30 minutes
Serves: 6
Net carbs: 10g
Fat: 21.7g
Protein: 2.3g

Ingredients:
- 1 medium onion
- 1 tsp. ground ginger
- 1 tsp. garlic
- 2 oz. (55g) butter
- 17 oz. (500g) pumpkin
- 2 cups (470 ml) vegetable stock
- 1 2/3 cups (400 ml) coconut cream
- Salt and pepper, to taste

Method:
1. Throw all the ingredients into your Instant pot and stir well.
2. Cover and set to the soup setting. Cook for 7 minutes.
3. Do a natural pressure release for ten minutes and then do a quick pressure release.
4. Open and blend with an immersion blender, adding more liquid if required.
5. Serve and enjoy!

Buffalo Chicken Soup

I just can't get enough of spice (as you might notice from the rest of this book), so I'm a big fan of this fast and tasty soup. Ready in less than 30 minutes, and with enough spice to blow your head off, it'll warm you from head to toe. Of course, dial down the spice if you like, or leave it out altogether. It's your soup.

Cooks: 20 mins
Serves: 6
Net carbs: 3.6g
Fat: 16g
Protein: 27g

Ingredients:
- 1 Tbsp. olive oil
- ½ large onion, diced
- ½ cup (112g) diced celery
- 4 cloves garlic, minced
- 1 lb. (450g) cooked chicken, shredded
- 4 cups (940ml) chicken broth
- 2-3 Tbsp. Buffalo sauce
- 6 oz. (170g) full-fate cream cheese, at room temperature, cubed
- ½ cup (120ml) heavy cream

Method:
1. Open up the Instant pot and add the oil. Set to sauté.
2. Throw in the onion and celery and cook for five minutes until soft. Add the garlic, stir for a minute then turn off.
3. Stir through the chicken, the broth and the buffalo sauce.
4. Cover and set to the soup setting. Cook for five minutes.
5. Do a natural pressure release for five minutes then do a quick pressure release.
6. Carefully place a small amount of the liquid into your blender with the cream cheese. Blend until smooth, adding more of the cooking liquid if required.
7. Pour back into the Instant pot, add the cream and stir until smooth.
8. Serve and enjoy!

Chicken Enchilada Soup

If you're a fan of authentic Mexican food, you'll love the well-rounded flavors of this Mexican enchilada soup. Combining cumin, chipotle, chili, onion, garlic, oregano, vinegar and salt, it creates the perfect balance of flavors which will keep you coming back for more. Yum!

Cooks: 30 minutes
Serves: 4
Net carbs: 8g
Fat: 10g
Protein: 29.9g

Ingredients:
- 1 Tbsp. olive oil
- 1 large yellow onion, diced
- 3 cloves garlic, minced
- 1 large red bell pepper, diced
- 1 large jalapeño, minced
- 1 cup (240 ml) sugar-free tomato sauce
- 1 Tbsp. chili powder
- 1 Tbsp. chipotle pepper in adobo sauce
- 2 tsp. ground cumin
- 1 tsp. garlic powder
- 1 tsp. onion powder
- 1 tsp. white wine vinegar
- 1 tsp. sea salt or pink Himalayan salt
- ½ tsp. oregano
- 3 cups (720 ml) chicken broth
- 1 lb. (450g) chicken breasts

To serve...
- Diced avocado, sliced jalapeno pepper, sour cream, minced cilantro

Method:
1. Place the oil into the Instant pot and set to sauté.
2. Add the onion, garlic, pepper and jalapeno pepper. Cook for 5 minutes until soft
3. Take a small bowl and add the tomato sauce, vinegar, chipotle and spices. Pour this on top of the onion mixture.

4. Stir through the broth and the chicken then cover.
5. Set to manual high and cook for 20 minutes.
6. Do a quick pressure release.
7. Remove the chicken carefully, shred then pop back into the pot. Stir well.
8. Serve and enjoy!

Broccoli & Cheese Soup

Broccoli and cheese. Need I say any more? It's nourishing, creamy, satisfying and amazing for any gathering or a simple dinner. Feel free to switch the cheeses if you prefer different types, or pile more in for added depth.

Cooks: 20 minutes
Serves: 10
Net carbs: 4.7g
Fat: 43g
Protein: 23.4g

Ingredients:

- 4 Tbsp. butter
- ½ onion, diced
- 3 garlic cloves minced
- 5 cups (1.1 liters) chicken broth
- 2 cups (450ml) heavy whipping cream
- 6 cups (540g) frozen broccoli florets
- 4 ¼ cups (560g) cheddar cheese
- 4 slices Swiss cheese
- 2 oz. (45g) cream cheese, softened and cubed
- ½ tsp. nutmeg
- 2 tsp. parsley
- 1 tsp. pink salt
- 1 tsp. black pepper
- 1 tsp. red pepper flakes (opt)
- ½ - ¾ tsp. Xanthan Gum

Method:

1. Place the butter, onions and garlic into the pan and cook on sauté for five minutes.
2. Add 3 cups (705ml) of the broth, and the broccoli, then bring to the boil.
3. Cover, set to manual and cook for five minutes.
4. Do a quick pressure release.
5. Add the remaining broth, cream, cream cheese and spices and stir well.
6. Set to sauté again, bring to the boil then add cheese.
7. Stir well and heat for a further five minutes.
8. Serve and enjoy.

Kimchi Beef Stew

This is one of those stews that will really surprise your guests when they come to join you for food. Incorporating rich Asian flavors but without any of the carbs, it tastes simply out of this world. You can leave out the tofu if you're not a big fan and add extra green onion if you'd like.

Cooks: 40 mins
Serves: 6
Net carbs: 7g
Fat: 8g
Protein: 22g

Ingredients:

- 2 cups (300g) Kimchi
- 1 lb. (450g) beef, cubed
- 1 cup (150g) chopped onion
- 1 cup (90g) mushrooms
- 1 Tbsp. minced garlic
- 1 Tbsp. minced ginger
- 1 Tbsp. sesame oil
- 1 Tbsp. dark soy sauce
- ½ tsp. cayenne pepper (or to taste)
- 1 Tbsp. red chili paste
- ¼ tsp. Splenda
- 2 cups (470ml) water
- Salt to taste

To serve...

- ½ cup (75g) diced green onion
- 1 cup (250g) firm tofu, diced

Method:

1. Place everything into the Instant pot and stir well.
2. Cover with the lid and set on high pressure. Cook for 15 minutes.
3. Do a natural pressure release for five minutes then do a quick pressure release for the rest.
4. Open up, add green onions and tofu and stir well.
5. Serve and enjoy.

Beef Curry Stew

Beef curry works incredibly well as a stew that will keep you charged and ready for ANYTHING all day long. Best of all, you can just throw it all into your Instant pot, set the timer and voila- it's ready.

Cooks: 40 mins
Serves: 6
Net carbs: 5g
Fat: 30g
Protein: 40g

Ingredients:

- 2.5 lb. (1.1 kg) beef stew chunks
- 1 lb. (450g) broccoli florets
- 3 zucchinis, chopped
- ½ cup (120ml) chicken broth (or use water)
- 2 Tbsp. curry powder
- 1 Tbsp. garlic power
- Salt to taste
- 14 oz. (400ml) can coconut milk

Method:

1. Open up your Instant pot and throw everything inside, starting with the beef.
2. Set to manual high pressure for 45 minutes.
3. Do a natural pressure release for 10 minutes then a quick pressure release.
4. Add the coconut milk and salt and stir.
5. Serve and enjoy!

Bacon Cheeseburger Soup

See? Told you I loved cheeseburgers!! This time, our old favorite makes a comeback as a rich and mouth-watering soup with everything you need to feel nourished inside and out!

Cooks: 20 minutes
Serves: 6
Net carbs: 10g
Fat: 26g
Protein: 29g

Ingredients:
- 6 oz. (170g) bacon, chopped
- 1 Tbsp. olive oil
- 1 ½ lb. (680g) hamburger meat
- 1 large onion, diced
- 2 stalks celery, diced
- 4 cups (1.2 kg) cauliflower, chopped
- 4 cups (940ml) beef broth
- 4 oz. (112g) cream cheese
- 1 cup (150g) shredded sharp cheddar cheese
- Sea salt, to taste

Method:
1. Place your olive oil into the Instant pot, set to sauté and cook the bacon. Remove from the pot and set to one side.
2. Repeat with the ground beef, cooking until brown. Remove.
3. Pop the veggies into the pot and soften for a few minutes.
4. Add the broth then cover.
5. Set to manual high pressure for 7 minutes, then do a quick release.
6. Use an immersion blender to puree.
7. Add the cheese, bacon and hamburger and stir well to combine.
8. Serve and enjoy!

Ground Beef and Cabbage Soup

Beef and cabbage are a soup combination that tastes a million times better than it sounds. When you get the seasoning just right, it will taste like a trip to Italy without the added weight gain! This recipe calls for coleslaw mix, but you can use any combination of cabbage, onion and carrots that you like. Just watch the carbs...

Cooks: 40 minutes
Serves: 14
Net carbs: 4g
Fat: 6g
Protein: 9g

Ingredients:
- 1 Tbsp. olive oil
- 1 large onion, chopped
- 1 lb. (450g) ground beef
- 1 tsp. each sea salt & pepper
- 1 lb. (450g) shredded coleslaw mix
- 1 x 15-oz. (425g) can diced tomatoes (with liquid)
- 6 cups (1.4 liters) beef broth
- 1 Tbsp. Italian seasoning
- ½ tsp. garlic powder
- 2 bay leaves

Method:
1. Set your Instant pot onto sauté and add the oil then the onions.
2. Cook for five minutes.
3. Add the ground beef and seasoning, stir well then turn the temperature to high. Cook for 10 minutes.
4. Turn off your Instant pot and add the remaining ingredients. Stir well.
5. Stir, cover and set to manual high pressure for 20 minutes.
6. Do a natural pressure release for five minutes then a quick pressure release.
7. Remove the bay leaves.
8. Serve and enjoy!

Beef Stew

Who says that you need potatoes to make a decent beef stew? Create this melt-in-the-mouth beef stew in your Instant pot and you'll feel like you've died and gone to heaven. If this is still too high carb for your needs, ditch the carrot and reduce the other veggies.

Cooks: 50 mins
Serves: 6
Net carbs: 6g
Fat: 20g
Protein: 20g

Ingredients:
- 1 ¼ lb. (555g) trimmed beef chuck roast, cubed (at room temp)
- 8 oz. (225g) whole mushrooms, quartered
- 6 oz. (170g) celery root, peeled and cubed
- 4 oz. (112g) pearl onions, trimmed and peeled
- 2-3 ribs celery, sliced
- 3 oz. (85g) carrot, sliced
- 2 cloves garlic, sliced
- 2 Tbsp. tomato paste
- 2 Tbsp. olive oil or bacon grease
- 5 cups (1.2 liters) beef broth
- 1 large bay leaf
- ½ tsp. dried thyme
- 1 tsp. oregano
- Salt and pepper, to taste

Method:
1. Add the oil into your Instant pot, turn onto sauté and add your mushrooms. Cook for two minutes then remove.
2. Add more oil to the pan and brown the beef.
3. Then add the bay leaf, thyme and tomato paste and stir well to cover the beef.
4. Cook for one minute, then add one cup (235ml) of the stock. Scrape off anything stuck to the bottom and stir through.
5. Add the rest of the broth and bring to the boil.
6. Cover and turn onto manual high for 30 minutes.
7. Do a natural pressure release for 10 minutes then a quick pressure release.
8. Serve and enjoy!

Poblano Chicken Soup

Yes! I know I said that beans are off the menu, but I only told a half-truth there. If you're more flexible about your diet and your carb count is low that day, you can indulge in a small portion every now and again, like the ones you'll find in this soup. If you're not a fan, eliminate the beans and double the cauliflower. It won't taste quite as good, but it will still be yum.

Cooks: 45 mins
Serves: 8
Net carbs: 8g
Fat: 5g
Protein: 22g

Ingredients:

- ½ cup (100g) navy beans soaked for an hour in hot water
- 1 cup (150g) diced onion
- 3 poblano peppers, chopped
- 5 cloves garlic
- 1 cup (100g) cauliflower, diced
- 1 ½ lb. (680g) chicken breast, large chunks
- ¼ cup (12.5g) cilantro, chopped
- 1 tsp. ground coriander
- 1 tsp. ground cumin
- 1-2 tsp. salt
- 2 ½ cups (585ml) water
- 2 oz. (55g) cream cheese

Method:

1. Throw everything (except the cream cheese) into your Instant pot and cover.
2. Set to manual high pressure and cook for 15 minutes.
3. Do a natural pressure release for ten minutes then do a quick pressure release.
4. Remove the chicken with tongs and place to one side.
5. Use an immersion blender to puree the soup, keeping some chunkiness for texture.
6. Switch your pot onto sauté and bring to the boil.
7. Stir through the cream cheese.
8. Shred the chicken and stir back into the pot. Warm until heated through.

Beef, Tomato and Cabbage Soup

Enjoy this beef, tomato and cabbage soup for that classic homemade taste with a dash of the exotic. Then curl up with a massive bowl of the stuff, tuck right in and remember how lucky you are to have a 'diet' like this.

Cooks: 30 minutes
Serves: 9
Net carbs: 4.3g
Fat: 14.8g
Protein: 15.6g

Ingredients:
- ½ small onion diced
- 2 garlic cloves minced
- 1 ½ lb. (680g) ground beef
- 3 cups (705ml) beef broth
- 1 x 14 oz. (400g) can diced tomatoes
- 1 x 8 oz. (225g) can tomato sauce
- 4 Tbsp. soy sauce
- 1 small cabbage, chopped
- 3 tsp. Worcestershire Sauce
- ½ tsp. parsley
- ½ tsp. salt
- ½ tsp. pepper

Method:
1. Turn your Instant pot onto sauté, add the oil and cook the onions and garlic for five minutes.
2. Next add the beef and cook until brown.
3. Add the remaining ingredients and stir well.
4. Cover with the lid and cook on manual high for 15 minutes.
5. Do a quick pressure release.
6. Serve and enjoy!

Low Carb Zuppa Toscana Soup

This soup is one of my all-time favorites. Nothing can compare to its creaminess, the hint of bacon, the satisfying ground sausage and that epic garlicky richness.

Cooks: 30 minutes
Serves: 5
Net carbs: 6g
Fat: 47g
Protein: 20g

Ingredients:
- 1 ¾ cups (240g) cooked ground sausage
- ½ cup (70g) cooked and diced bacon
- ¼ cup (25g) diced shallots
- 1 tsp. minced garlic
- 4 cups (940ml) chicken broth
- 1 cup (100g) diced cauliflower
- 2 cups (130g) chopped kale
- ¾ cups (180ml) heavy whipping cream

Method:
1. Turn your Instant pot onto sauté, add the oil and cook the onions and garlic for five minutes.
2. Next add the sausage, bacon, broth and cauliflower and stir well.
3. Cover with the lid and cook on manual high pressure for 15 minutes.
4. Do a quick pressure release.
5. Stir through the kale and the cream.
6. Serve and enjoy!

Mexican Chicken Soup

Imagine if you could take a regular spiced chicken soup and give it a facelift so it tastes even more amazing and satisfying whilst sticking to the Keto principles. Yes, that's exactly what you have here. Spice, heat, flavor and creaminess...

Cooks: 45 minutes
Serves: 4
Net Carbs: 8g
Fat: 20g
Protein: 38g

Ingredients:

- 1 lb. (400g) boneless skinless chicken breast
- 10.5 oz. (300g) plum tomato Fire-roasted
- 1 medium onion
- 1 Tbsp. minced garlic
- 1 red bell pepper
- 1 tsp. cumin
- 1 tsp. oregano
- 1 ½ tsp. chipotle chili powder
- 1 tsp. paprika
- 1 tsp. Mexican Seasoning
- 1 ½ cups (350ml) chicken stock
- 1 cup (240ml) cream
- ½ cup (120ml) cream cheese
- 1 cup (150g) Cheddar cheese
- Salt to taste
- 1 tsp. butter
- Fresh Cilantro leaves for garnishing

Method:

1. Turn your Instant pot onto sauté, add the oil and cook the onions and garlic for five minutes.
2. Next add the chicken, tomatoes, spices, salt and chicken stock. Stir well.
3. Cover with the lid and cook on manual high pressure for 30 minutes.
4. Do a quick pressure release.
5. Open and add the bell peppers, cream, cream cheese and shredded cheese.
6. Stir well then replace the lid.
7. Cook on manual high for 5 minutes then do a quick pressure release.
8. Serve and enjoy!

Italian Sausage Soup

It always amazes me how a few handfuls of carefully-chosen herbs can transform a meal from good to awesome. My favorites are basil and oregano as they take me back to long evenings in the Italian countryside, laughing with friends and drinking copious bottles of local wine. The trip has gone but this delicious soup remains. Enjoy!

Cooks: 45 mins
Serves: 6
Net cabs: 7g
Fat: 20g
Protein: 20g

Ingredients:

- 1 lb. (450g) ground Italian sausage
- 4 oz. (112g) onion
- 2 stalks celery
- 2 oz. (56g) carrot (can eliminate to further reduce carbs)
- 15 oz. (425g) tomato sauce
- 2 cloves garlic
- 32 oz. (950ml) beef broth
- 1 Tbsp. fresh basil
- ¼ tsp. dried oregano
- ¼ tsp. red pepper flakes
- ¼ tsp. black pepper
- ½ tsp. sea salt
- Optional: additional basil

Method:

1. Turn your Instant pot onto sauté, add the oil and cook the onions and garlic for five minutes.
2. Next add the sausage and cook until brown.
3. Add the remaining ingredients and stir well.
4. Cover with the lid and cook on manual high pressure for 30 minutes.
5. Do a quick pressure release then serve and enjoy!

Hungarian Goulash

Whenever I've had a terrible day, or the weekend can't come fast enough, I head to the kitchen and create a big pot full of this Keto-friendly goulash. The combination of garlic, caraway seeds and paprika makes a welcome, warming change and the veggies as just enough balance to make it oh-so moreish.

Cooks: 45 minutes
Serves: 8
Net carbs: 5.52g
Fats: 23g
Protein: 23g

Ingredients:
- 2 Tbsp. bacon grease or lard (or butter)
- 1 cup (150g) chopped onion
- 2 Tbsp. Hungarian paprika
- 2 cloves garlic
- 2 lb. (900g) beef stew meat, cubed
- 1 tsp. salt
- ½ tsp. pepper
- ½ tsp. caraway seeds
- 2 cups (220g) daikon radish, cubed
- 1 yellow or green pepper, chopped
- 2 stalks celery, sliced
- 1 x 15 oz. can diced tomatoes
- 1 ½ cups (350ml) chicken or beef broth
- 1 bay leaf

Method:
1. Turn your Instant pot onto sauté, add the oil and cook the onions and garlic for five minutes.
2. Add the paprika and stir for a minute.
3. Next add the beef and cook until brown.
4. Add the remaining ingredients and stir well.
5. Cover with the lid and turn onto manual high pressure for 30 minutes.
6. Do a natural pressure release for 10 minutes then a quick pressure release.
7. Serve and enjoy!

Low Carb Vegetable Soup

Just because you're following a Keto diet, that doesn't mean that you have to deprive yourself of veggie soup. This one is simple, nutritious and absolutely scrumptious. Lower the carb content further by omitting the turnip and carrot.

Cooks: 30 minutes
Serves: 12
Net carbs: 10g
Protein: 3g
Fat: 1g

Ingredients:

- 1 large turnip cubed
- 1 small onion chopped
- 6 stalks celery chopped
- 1 medium carrot chopped (optional)
- 15 oz. (425g) pumpkin puree
- 1 lb. (450g) green beans frozen or fresh
- 64 oz. (1.9l) chicken broth
- 2 cups (470ml) water
- 1 Tbsp. fresh basil chopped (or 1.5 teaspoons dried)
- ¼ tsp. thyme leaves
- 1/8 tsp. rubbed sage
- Salt, to taste
- 1 lb. (450g) spinach leaves chopped (fresh or frozen)

Method:

1. Place all of the ingredients into your Instant pot and stir well.
2. Cover and cook on manual high for ten minutes.
3. Do a natural pressure release for 10 minutes.
4. Open and stir through the spinach.
5. Serve and enjoy!

Greek Lemon Chicken Soup

When it's hot outside and you want a light meal or a starter with a difference, hop into the kitchen and make this citrussy, luxurious chicken soup. I promise you'll keep coming back for more!

Cooks: 35 mins
Serves: 4
Net carbs: 4g
Fat: 10.75g
Protein: 17.8g

Ingredients:

- 2 Tbsp. olive oil separated
- 2 large chicken breasts, cubed into bite-size chunks
- 1 medium onion finely diced
- 2 large celery stalks diced
- 4 garlic cloves minced
- 4 cups (940ml) chicken broth
- Zest of a lemon
- ½ tsp. salt
- ¼ tsp. fresh cracked black pepper
- 1 bay leaf
- 1 free-range egg
- Juice of a lemon
- Salt and pepper, to taste
- Fresh parsley, to garnish (optional)

Method:

1. Turn your Instant pot onto sauté, add half of the oil and cook the chicken until brown. Remove and pop to one side.
2. Next add the remaining oil and add the onions, celery and garlic. Cook for five minutes.
3. Pop the chicken back into the pot and add the remaining ingredients, apart from the eggs and lemon juice.
4. Cover and cook on manual high for 20 minutes.
5. Do a natural pressure release for 3 minutes, then do a quick pressure release.
6. Take bowl and whisk the eggs and lemon together.

7. Carefully remove some of the broth from the Instant pot and gently (and slowly!) add to the egg mixture. Stir until smooth.
8. Pour into the Instant pot and stir well until combined.
9. Serve and enjoy!

Jalapeno Popper Soup

Don't let the big list of ingredients put you off- it's all for a very good cause. And besides, it's not quite as bad as it looks and it's well worth the effort. Creamy, spicy and chickeny (is that even a word??), it's amazing.

Serves: 8
Cooks: 30 minutes
Net carbs: 2.1g
Fat: 40.1g
Protein: 41.2g

Ingredients:
- 1 ½ lb. boneless skinless chicken breasts
- 3 Tbsp. butter
- 2 garlic cloves minced
- ½ onion chopped
- ½ green pepper chopped
- 2 jalapenos seeded and chopped
- ½ lb. (225g) bacon cooked and crumbled
- 6 oz. (170g) cream cheese
- 3 cups (705 ml) chicken broth
- ½ cup (120ml) heavy whipping cream
- ¼ tsp. paprika
- 1 tsp. cumin
- 1 tsp. salt
- ½ tsp. pepper
- ¾ cup (90g) Monterrey Jack cheese
- ¾ cup (90g) Cheddar cheese
- ½ tsp. xanthan gum

Method:
1. Turn your Instant pot onto sauté, add the oil and cook the onions, green pepper, jalapenos and seasoning. Cook for five minutes.
2. Next add the chicken, cream cheese and broth.
3. Stir well to combine.
4. Set the Instant pot to manual high and cook for 15 minutes.
5. Do a natural pressure release for 5 minutes, then do a quick pressure release.

6. Remove the chicken from the pot, shred and return.
7. Add the cream, cheese and cooked bacon and stir until the cheese melts.
8. Add the xanthan gum and turn onto the warm setting.
9. Heat for a few minutes then serve and enjoy!

Meat Chicken

Garlic Chipotle Lime Chicken

Don't you just love recipes that sound like they'd fit in a gourmet restaurant but turn out to be simple? Yep, me too. This one is one of my favorites. Just whizz the sauce ingredients in a blender, throw into your pot with the chicken and you're practically done.

Cooks: 30 minutes
Serves: 6
Net carbs: 2g
Fats: 9g
Protein: 22g

Ingredients:
For the chicken...
- 1 ½ lb. chicken breasts or thighs boneless skinless

For the sauce...
- 1/3 cup (160g) tomato sauce
- 2 Tbsp. olive oil
- 2 cloves garlic
- 2 Tbsp. mild green chilies, canned
- 1 Tbsp. apple cider vinegar
- 3 Tbsp. lime juice
- 1/3 cup (8g) fresh cilantro or flat leaf Italian parsley
- 1 ½ tsp. sweetener of choice: Swerve or coconut sugar
- 1 tsp. ground chipotle powder mild to spicy
- 1 tsp. sea salt
- ¼ tsp. black pepper

Method:
1. Start by making your super-easy sauce. Place the sauce ingredients into your blender and hit blend until smooth.
2. Pour into your Instant pot.
3. Add the chicken breasts, cover and cook on manual high for 20 minutes.
4. Do a quick pressure release and stir well.
5. Add more liquid as required.
6. Serve and enjoy!

Spaghetti Squash Chicken Alfredo

Spaghetti squash really hits the spot when it comes to noodle cravings. They're light, delicious and work amazingly well with the Chicken Alfredo. Who said Keto had to be boring, right?

Cooks: 30 minutes
Serves: 5
Net carbs: 6g
Fats: 19g
Protein: 32g

Ingredients:
- 1 whole spaghetti squash
- 1 lb. (450g) skinless chicken breasts
- 4 oz. (112g) reduced-fat cream cheese
- ½ cup (120ml) low-sodium chicken broth
- 2 cups (180g) broccoli
- 1 cup (120g) parmesan cheese
- ¼ cup (60ml) heavy whipping cream
- ¾ Tbsp. butter
- 1 Tbsp. minced garlic
- 2 cups (470ml) milk
- 1 cup (235ml) water
- 1 tsp. olive oil
- McCormick's Grill Mates Montreal Chicken Seasoning
- Salt and pepper, to taste
- 1 cup (235ml) water

Method:
1. Place the water into the bottom of your Instant pot.
2. Cut the squash in half, scoop out the seeds and place into the Instant pot, with the cut side up.
3. Cover with the lid and cook on manual high for 7 minutes.
4. Do a quick pressure release and check that the squash is cooked.
5. Shred with a fork and pop to one side.
6. Pour away the water from the squash and switch onto sauté. Add the olive oil to the pot.

7. Take your chicken, season well and place into the Instant pot. Cook on both sides until brown. Remove from the Instant pot and place to one side.
8. Add the garlic to the pan and stir well, scraping any brown bits from the bottom of your pot.
9. Add the broth and keep stirring.
10. Grab a bowl and add the milk, cream, cream cheese, butter and flour or xanthan gum. Stir well and add to Instant pot.
11. Serve and enjoy!

Creamy Salsa Chicken

LOVE. THIS. RECIPE! Just six ingredients, a dose of love and thirty minutes cooking time and you can have this awesome chicken ready, steaming hot and ready to serve the troops.

Cooks: 30 mins
Serves: 6
Net carbs: 4g
Fat: 12g
Protein: 43g

Ingredients:
- 3 lb. (1.4kg) chicken breasts
- ½ cup (117ml) chicken broth
- 4 oz. (112g) cream cheese
- ½ cup (112g) cottage cheese
- 1 cup (260g) salsa
- 1-2 tsp. taco or fajita seasoning

Method:
1. Start by placing the chicken and the broth into the Instant Pot.
2. Cover, pop your Instant pot onto the poultry setting and cook for 10 minutes.
3. Do a quick pressure release and check that the chicken is cooked. If not, return to the Instant pot and cook for a further 5-10 minutes.
4. Remove the chicken and place into a bowl. Throw away half of the cooking liquid.
5. Put the Instant pot back onto sauté and add the remaining ingredients. Whisk until combined and allow the cheese to melt.
6. Shred the chicken and add back into the pot.
7. Serve and enjoy!

Cool Ranch Chicken

This mouth-watering chicken recipe is incredibly simple to make, it's packed with flavor and you will LOVE how it practically melts in your mouth. Yummy!

Cooks: 30 minutes
Serves: 6-8
Net carbs: 3g
Fat: 6g
Protein: 30g

Ingredients:
- 2 lb. (900g) boneless skinless chicken breasts
- 2 Tbsp. ranch seasoning (choose no-sugar)
- 2 Tbsp. taco seasoning (choose no-sugar)
- 1 Tbsp. olive oil
- 1 Tbsp. red wine vinegar
- ¾ cup (180ml) chicken broth

Method:
1. Start by combining the seasonings, oil, vinegar and broth in a small bowl. Whisk
2. Place the chicken into the bottom of the Instant pot and pour over the seasoning mixture.
3. Cover and set to manual high for 15 minutes.
4. Do a natural pressure release.
5. Remove the chicken, shred and return back to the pot.
6. Stir well, then serve and enjoy!

Coconut Curry Chicken

Whenever I smell that delicious scent of coconut milk, it reminds me of my grandfather. He was stationed in India during the war and came home blessed with the knowledge of how to make the most amazing curries on this planet. This recipe comes pretty close.

Cooks: 1 hour
Serves: 5
Net carbs: 5.6g
Fat: 29g
Protein: 26.4g

Ingredients:

- 5 raw boneless and skinless chicken thighs
- 1 can (400ml) coconut milk
- 1 cup (235ml) chicken broth
- 2 ½ Tbsp. butter
- 1 Tbsp. curry powder
- 3 cloves garlic
- 1 tsp. grated ginger
- ½ tsp. cinnamon
- ½ tsp. salt
- ¼ medium red onion

Method:

1. Turn your Instant pot onto sauté, add the oil and cook the chicken until browned.
2. Next add the onions, garlic, ginger, curry powder and cinnamon. Cook for 2-3 minutes.
3. Add the remaining ingredients and stir well.
4. Cover with the lid and turn onto manual high for 20 minutes.
5. Do a quick pressure release.
6. Serve and enjoy!

Rosemary Chicken with Bacon & Cheese

There used to be the biggest rosemary bush outside my apartment. Every day, I'd walk past and pinch off just a tiny bit so I could get that fresh herb flavor for free. Because of this, tons of my recipes now contain the herb, like this one. Combined with the flavor of the spices and the rich cream, I know you'll love it from that very first bite!

Cooks: 30 minutes
Serves: 8
Net carbs: 2.5g
Fat: 24.7g
Protein: 17.2g

Ingredients:
- 4-6 boneless skinless chicken breasts (depending on how many people you are serving)
- 2 Tbsp. butter
- ½ tsp. poultry seasoning
- ½ tsp. rosemary
- 1/8 tsp. thyme
- 1 tsp. dried garlic
- ¾ cup (180ml) chicken broth
- 6 pieces bacon
- 2/3 cup (160ml) heavy whipping cream
- 2 oz. (56g) cream cheese
- ¾ tsp. xanthan gum
- 1 cup (125g) shredded cheese
- 3 pieces bacon crumbled
- Salt & pepper, to taste

Method:
1. Turn your Instant pot onto sauté, add the butter and cook the bacon until crispy. Remove ½ of the bacon.
2. Next add the chicken and the seasoning, rosemary, thyme, garlic and broth.
3. Cover and set to manual high pressure for 11 minutes.
4. Do a natural pressure release for 6 minutes, then a quick pressure release.
5. Remove the chicken and shred. Return to the pot.

6. Switch the Instant pot onto sauté and add the cream and cream cheese. Stir well to combine.
7. Add the xanthan gum, stir well and then cover with cheese and the remaining bacon.
8. Serve and enjoy!

Garlic and Spinach Chicken

Another super simple recipe that really delivers on the nutrition. With the addition of spinach and fragrant turmeric, this recipe is absolutely incredible, perfect for picnics, great to use in salads the following day and even great nibbled straight from the fridge. Yum!

Cooks: 40 mins
Serves: 4
Net carbs: 3g
Fat: 18g
Protein: 28g

Ingredients:

- 4 chicken breasts, whole or chopped
- 1 cup (235ml) chicken broth
- 4 Tbsp. ghee or melted butter
- 1 tsp. turmeric powder
- 1 tsp. salt
- 10 cloves garlic, peeled and diced
- A handful of spinach, to taste

Method:

1. Pop the ghee into the Instant pot and add the chicken. Cook until browned.
2. Add the garlic, turmeric, salt and broth.
3. Cover and set to manual high pressure for 30 minutes.
4. Do a manual pressure release for 5 minutes then do a quick pressure release.
5. Remove the chicken and shred, then return to the pot.
6. Stir through the spinach and then serve and enjoy.

Chicken with Creamy Mushroom Gravy

Mushrooms are popular with Keto-aficionados as they're a great extra source of protein, they're really low carb and they contain an incredible amount of folate, zinc, iron and most of the B-vitamins too. Pimp them up in a creamy sauce, add the chicken and get ready to have your taste buds astonished.

Cooks: 35 mins
Serves: 2
Net carbs: 10g
Fat: 38g
Protein: 60g

Ingredients:

- 2 boneless skinless chicken breasts (about 1 lb./450g total)
- 10 oz. (280g) cremini mushrooms, sliced
- 1 Tbsp. olive oil
- 1 Tbsp. chopped fresh parsley
- Salt and pepper, to taste

For the gravy...

- ½ cup (120ml) heavy whipping cream
- ½ cup (117ml) water
- ½ cup (60g) finely grated Parmesan cheese
- 1 Tbsp. xanthan gum
- 1 tsp. garlic powder
- 1/8 tsp. or less cayenne powder

Method:

1. Turn your Instant pot onto sauté, add the olive oil and then add the mushrooms.
2. Add the cream, water, garlic and cayenne. Stir well then turn off.
3. Season the chicken with salt and pepper, then place into the Instant pot. Make sure they're in the liquid itself.
4. Cover and set to manual high pressure for 6 minutes.
5. Do a natural pressure release for five minutes, then do a quick pressure release.
6. Pop the chicken breasts on the serving plate.
7. Stir the Parmesan into the sauce and sprinkle over the xanthan gum. Stir until thickens.
8. Serve and enjoy.

Sweet & Spicy Barbecue Chicken Wings

Good news- you can still eat spicy BBQ sauce when you're following Keto. You just need to switch some of the ingredients and you'll have an explosion of taste that will satisfy your taste buds and keep your tummy happy too.

Cooks: 30 mins
Serves: 6
Net carbs: 1.6g
Fat: 19.5g
Protein: 27.2g

Ingredients:
For the barbeque sauce...
- 1 tsp. liquid smoke
- 4 oz. (112g) tomato paste
- 4 Tbsp. Frank's Red-Hot Sauce
- ½ cup (120ml) apple cider vinegar
- ½ cup (120ml) water
- 1/8 tsp. ground cayenne pepper
- 1/8 tsp. ground chipotle chili
- ¼ tsp. crushed red pepper flakes
- ½ tsp. paprika
- 1 tsp. cinnamon
- 1 tsp. salt
- 1 tsp. sweetener (or more, to taste)

For the chicken wings...
- 2 lb. (900g) chicken wings
- 1 Tbsp. coarse salt

Method:
1. Start by placing the sauce ingredients into the Instant pot and switching to sauté. Simmer for 5 minutes.
2. Next place the chicken into a bowl, cover with the salt and coat well.
3. Pop the chicken into the sauce in the Instant pot.
4. Cover and set to manual high pressure for 10 minutes.
5. Do a quick pressure release.
6. Remove the chicken and place under a broiler for 10 minutes, turning half way through.
7. Serve and enjoy!

Lemon and Garlic Chicken Legs

Lemon and garlic chicken is such an incredible meal that I believe EVERYONE should add it to the menu at least one per week. Taking just 30 minutes, they'll be ready and on the table in no time!

Cooks: 30 mins
Serves: 4
Net Carbs: 3g
Fat: 9g
Protein: 30g

Ingredients:

- 2 lb. (900g) frozen chicken legs
- 1 tsp. salt
- ¼ tsp. pepper
- 1 tsp. Italian herbs seasoning
- 1 lemon, quartered
- 8 garlic cloves, peeled
- 1 cup (235ml) water

Method:

1. Place the water into the bottom of the Instant and add the garlic, salt, pepper and Italian herbs. Stir well to combine.
2. Place the chicken into the liquid, top with the lemon and cover.
3. Set to manual high pressure and cook for 25 minutes.
4. Do a quick pressure release.
5. Serve and enjoy.

Parmesan and Asiago Fried Chicken

That's right- you can also create 'fried chicken' in your Instant pot and it tastes pretty good too. You'll love this recipe if you're a big cheese fan or you want a simple meal that will definitely impress. Give it a try.

Cooks: 45 minutes
Serves: 6
Net carbs: 0g
Fat: 17g
Protein: 41g

Ingredients:
- 3-4 boneless skinless chicken breasts
- 1 free-range egg
- 2 Tbsp. water
- ¾ cup Asiago cheese
- 6 Tbsp. grated Parmesan cheese
- ¼ tsp. garlic powder
- ¼ tsp. pepper
- ½ tsp. salt
- 2-4 Tbsp. olive oil
- 4 slices bacon, cooked and crumbled

Method:
1. Start by mixing the egg and water in a bowl.
2. Take another bowl and mix the dry ingredients. Place ¼ of this mixture to one side.
3. Dip the chicken in the egg mixture, then the dry mixture, coating well.
4. Place the oil into the bottom of the Instant Pot and place the chicken inside. Cook until browned.
5. Cover with the lid and cook on manual high pressure for 20 minutes.
6. Do a quick pressure release.
7. Remove the chicken and place into the broiler for five minutes until browned.
8. Serve and enjoy!

Creamy Garlic Tuscan Chicken Thighs

Thanks to the addition of cream, cheese, tomatoes, herbs and spinach, this chicken recipe really dials up the Italian flavor and gives you a taste of the sunshine even when it's dull and cloudy outside. Yum!

Cooks: 35 mins
Serves: 4
Net Carbs: 4g
Fat: 14g
Protein: 17g

Ingredients:
- 4 chicken thighs
- 4 oz. (112g) cream cheese
- 2 ½ cups (565g) spinach
- ¼ cup (15g) sundried tomatoes
- 1 Tbsp. chicken seasoning
- ¼ cup (30g) Parmesan cheese
- 3 garlic cloves
- 1 tsp. olive oil
- 1 cup (235ml) low-sodium chicken broth
- 1 cup (235ml) milk
- 2 Tbsp. heavy whipping cream
- 2 tsp. Italian Seasoning
- 1 tsp. xanthan gum
- 1 tsp. water
- Salt and pepper, to taste
- Fresh parsley

Method:
1. Turn your Instant pot onto sauté and add the olive oil.
2. Season the chicken with 1 teaspoon of seasoning plus the salt and pepper.
3. Place into the Instant pot and brown.
4. Next add the milk, broth, and remaining seasoning.
5. Cover and cook on manual high pressure for 15 minutes.
6. Do a quick pressure release.
7. Remove the chicken and pop to one side.

8. Add the cream cheese, sundried tomatoes, cream, parmesan, garlic and spinach to the pot. Stir well.
9. Set Instant pot to sauté and warm through.
10. Sprinkle with Xanthan gum and stir until thickened.
11. Serve and enjoy!

Coconut Chicken

This coconut chicken has such a well-rounded flavor that it's hard to believe it came right from your Instant pot. This recipe calls for leftover cooked chicken, but you could easily increase the cooking time and use raw chicken instead. And as with any curry recipe, it tastes even better the next day!

Cooks: 15 minutes
Serves: 4
Net carbs: 5g
Fat: 15g
Protein: 9g

Ingredients:
- 1 onion, chopped
- 2 cloves garlic
- 3 cups (525g) green bell pepper
- 1 ½ tsp. salt
- 1 Tbsp. garam masala
- 1 Tbsp. curry powder
- 2 Tbsp. almond butter
- 1 x 10 oz. (295ml) canned coconut milk
- 8 oz. (225g) tomato paste
- 3 ¾ cups (470g) cooked chicken, diced
- 1 cup (235ml) water

Method:
1. Place all the ingredients except the chicken and water into a blender. Whizz until smooth.
2. Now place the chicken into your Instant pot, cover with the sauce and add the water.
3. Cover and cook on manual high pressure for 10 minutes.
4. Do a natural pressure release for five minutes, then a quick pressure release.
5. Serve and enjoy!

Belizean Stewed Chicken

Let's fly over to the Caribbean to try that unique flavor of Belizean chicken. This recipe calls for 'achiote seasoning' which is basically a blend of paprika, cumin and oregano. If you don't have any near you, feel free to substitute with paprika or mild chili.

Cooks: 45 minutes
Serves: 8
Net carbs: 3g
Fat: 22g
Protein: 28g

Ingredients:
- 4 whole chicken legs
- 1 Tbsp. olive oil
- 2 Tbsp. achiote seasoning
- 2 Tbsp. white vinegar
- 3 Tbsp. soy sauce
- 1 cup (150g) sliced yellow onions
- 3 cloves garlic, sliced
- 1 tsp. ground cumin
- 1 tsp. dried oregano
- ½ tsp. ground black pepper
- 1 Tbsp. granulated sugar substitute
- 2 cups (470ml) chicken stock

Method:
1. Start by placing the achiote paste, vinegar, soy sauce, cumin, oregano, pepper and sweetener in a bowl and stirring well.
2. Place the chicken into this marinade and pop into the fridge for marinate for at least an hour, preferable overnight.
3. Switch your Instant pot onto sauté and add the olive oil.
4. Place the chicken into the Instant pot and cook until brown. Remove and set to one side.
5. Next pop the onions and garlic into the Instant pot and sauté for 2-3 minutes until soft.
6. Return the chicken to the pot and add the chicken stock.
7. Cover, set to manual high pressure and cook for 20 minutes.
8. Do a quick pressure release.
9. Serve and enjoy!

Buffalo Chicken Cauliflower

Bring on the buffalo chicken with cauliflower! It helps pack in a vitamin C punch, it's deliciously satisfying, and it will be ready super-fast. As it's made using precooked chicken, it's great way to use up leftovers or ideal when you're pressed for time but want to keep nutrition to a high.

Cooks: 15 mins
Serves: 6
Net carbs: 7.7g
Fat: 25g
Protein: 24g

Ingredients:

- 1 head cauliflower
- 2 cups (250g) cooked chicken
- ½ cup (110g) Buffalo sauce
- ¼ cup (60ml) Ranch dressing
- 4 oz. (112g) cream cheese
- 2 cups (250g) shredded cheddar cheese
- Salt & pepper, to taste

Method:

1. Place the cauliflower, chicken, seasoning, sauce and dressing into your Instant pot. Stir well.
2. Cover and cook on manual high for 5 minutes.
3. Do a natural pressure release for five minutes then do a quick pressure release.
4. Open and stir through the cream cheese and cheddar.
5. Serve and enjoy!

Chicken Cacciatore

This recipe is perfect for those days when you open your pantry and realize that you have barely anything inside apart from an onion, some spices and a couple of chilis. THAT'S when the magic happens. THAT'S when you create perfect meals like this...

Cooks: 15 mins
Serves: 6
Net carbs: 7 g
Fat: 2g
Protein: 18g

Ingredients:

- 24 oz. (680g) low sugar spaghetti sauce (can substitute with canned tomatoes)
- 4 chicken breasts boneless skinless, cut into bite size pieces
- ½ onion
- 3 bell peppers any variety
- ½ tsp. chili powder
- 1 tsp. garlic salt
- ½ cup (120ml) water

Method:

1. Place the chicken, spaghetti sauce or tomatoes and water into your Instant pot. Stir well.
2. Add the peppers, onions, chili powder and garlic salt. Stir well again.
3. Cover and cook on manual high pressure for 5 minutes.
4. Do a natural pressure release for 5 minutes then a quick pressure release.
5. Serve and enjoy!

Chicken Piccata

Heavy on the oregano, basil and capers, this chicken recipe is perfect to come home to when you want comfort food with a difference. It's also simple and tastes even better the next day. If you can bear to wait that long.

Cooks: 30 mins
Serves: 4
Net carbs: 3g
Fat: 8g
Protein: 42g

Ingredients:

- 1 Tbsp. olive oil
- 2 lb. (900g) boneless skinless chicken breasts
- Salt and pepper, to taste
- 1 clove garlic, minced
- ¾ cup (180ml) reduced-sodium chicken stock
- ¼ cup (60ml) fresh lemon juice
- 1 tsp. dried oregano
- 1 tsp. dried basil
- 4 oz. (112g) capers, drained

Method:

1. Turn your Instant pot onto sauté and add the oil.
2. Season the chicken and then place into the Instant pot. Cook for a few minutes each side until browned.
3. Removed the chicken and then place onto a plate.
4. Add the garlic to the pot and stir, then add the broth, lemon juice, oregano and basil, and scrape the bottom of the pot.
5. Pop the chicken back inside the pot, sprinkle with capers and cover.
6. Cook on manual high for 10 minutes.
7. Do a quick pressure release.
8. Serve and enjoy!

Roasted Rotisserie Chicken

Yes, you CAN roast chicken in your Instant pot and it WILL taste better than you could have ever imagined. Just throw it all in, head off to do something fun and you're done! Bon Appetit!

Cooks: 45 mins
Serves: 4
Net carbs: 3g
Fat: 8g
Protein: 10g

Ingredients:
For the chicken...
- 4 lb. chicken, whole
- 1 lemon
- 1 onion, quartered
- 1 cup (235ml) water

For the rotisserie seasoning...
- 1 Tbsp. kosher salt
- 2 tsp. pepper
- 1 Tbsp. garlic powder
- 1 Tbsp. onion powder
- 1 Tbsp. paprika
- 1 tsp. dried thyme
- Dash of cayenne pepper

Method:
1. Start by making the seasoning. Place all the seasoning ingredients into a bowl and stir well.
2. Place the cut lemon and onion into the cavity of the chicken and pat well with the seasoning.
3. Then open your Instant pot and pour in the water. Place the trivet inside.
4. Lower the chicken onto the trivet and cover.
5. Cook on manual high for 25 minutes.
6. Do a natural pressure release for 10 minutes, then a quick pressure release.
7. Serve and enjoy!

Indian Butter Chicken

Lightly spiced Indian chicken in tomato sauce is another of my go-to recipes. I love the way it combines individual spices to create a well-blended flavor that is authentic and delicious. If you don't have the spices or you can't be bothered measuring it all out, simply substitute for regular curry powder.

Cooks: 25 mins
Serves: 4
Net carbs: 2g
Fat: 20g
Protein: 25g

Ingredients:

- 1 x 14 oz. (400g) can diced tomatoes
- 5-6 cloves garlic
- 1-2 tsp. minced ginger
- 1 tsp. turmeric
- ½ tsp. cayenne pepper
- 1 tsp. paprika
- 1 tsp. salt
- 1 tsp. garam masala
- 1 tsp. ground cumin
- 1 lb. (450g) boneless skinless chicken thighs

To serve...

- 4 oz. (112g) butter
- 4 oz. (112g) heavy cream
- 1 tsp. garam masala
- ¼ - ½ cup chopped cilantro

Method

1. Open up the Instant pot and add all ingredients. Stir well.
2. Cover and cook on manual high pressure for 10 minutes.
3. Do a natural pressure release for 10 minutes then a quick pressure release.
4. Open the pot, remove the chicken and place to one side.
5. Use an immersion blender to puree the sauce.
6. Allow to cool slightly then add the butter, cream, cilantro and garam masala and stir well.
7. Pop the chicken back into the pot and stir well to coat.
8. Serve and enjoy!

Chicken Chili No Beans

If you've even been sooo desperate to eat chili but you can't face picking out all the beans, then listen up. I have the recipe for you. This one is authentically delicious but keeps the carbs at a healthy 3 grams, so you can still enjoy the flavor on the Keto diet.

Cooks: 40 minutes
Serves: 8
Net carbs: 3g
Fat: 12g
Protein: 20g

Ingredients:

- 1 ½ lb. (680g) frozen chicken breast
- 8 oz. (225g) cream cheese
- ½ tsp. cumin
- 2 tsp. salt
- 20 oz. (590ml) chicken broth
- ½ tsp. chili powder
- ½ tsp. pepper
- 10 oz. (280g) diced tomatoes with green chilies
- 4 ½ oz. (127g) canned green chilis, shredded

To serve...
- Mexican cheese, avocado and sour cream

Method:

1. Open the Instant pot and throw all the ingredients (apart from the cream cheese) inside.
2. Cover and cook on manual high pressure for 15 minutes.
3. Do a natural pressure release for 15 minutes, then a quick pressure release.
4. Open up and remove the chicken, placing it onto a plate and shred.
5. Stir the chicken back into the pot.
6. Add the cream cheese and stir through.
7. Serve and enjoy.

Taiwanese Three Cup Chicken (San Bei Ji)

A word of warning- this is one of those recipes that gets addictive after just a bite or two. It's fragrant, it's satisfying and it's brilliantly Asian. Love it! So will you!

Cooks: 10 mins
Serves: 6
Net carbs: 6g
Fat: 15g
Protein: 31g

Ingredients:
- 4 Tbsp. sesame oil
- 6 dried red chilis
- 4 Tbsp. smashed garlic cloves
- 2 Tbsp. ginger, sliced
- 2 lb. (900g) boneless skinless chicken thighs, halved
- 4 Tbsp. soy sauce
- 4 Tbsp. rice wine
- Salt to taste

To serve...
- ¼ cup Thai basil chopped, or regular basil
- ½ tsp. xanthan gum

Method:
1. Turn the Instant pot to sauté and add the oil then the chilis, ginger and garlic. Fry for 2 mins.
2. Then add everything else and stir well.
3. Cover and cook on manual high pressure for 7 minutes.
4. Do a natural pressure release for 10 minutes then quick release the rest.
5. Open and turn onto sauté, then add the basil leaves, stirring well.
6. Sprinkle the xanthan gum over the liquid and stir well to combine.
7. Serve and enjoy!

Jamaican Chicken Curry

The first time I tried Jamaican food I knew I'd found a winner because their food is exactly how I like it. Spicy, fragrant, flecked with oregano, and HOT! You can make a milder version by getting rid of the chili, using mild curry powder and using less allspice. But where would be the fun in that??

Cooks: 20 mins
Serves: 4
Net carbs: 3g
Fat: 11g
Protein: 23g

Ingredients:
- 2 Tbsp. oil
- 1 Tbsp. minced ginger
- 1 Tbsp. minced garlic
- 1 cup (150g) chopped onion
- 1 ½ Tbsp. Jamaican Curry Powder
- 1 scotch bonnet pepper sliced
- 3 sprigs fresh thyme or 1/2 teaspoon dried thyme
- 1 tsp. salt
- ½ tsp. ground allspice
- 1 lb. (450g) boneless skinless chicken thighs cut into 3 pieces each
- ½ cup (120ml) water

Method:
1. Turn the Instant pot onto sauté and add the oil. Add the onion, garlic and ginger, and cook for a couple of minutes.
2. Throw in the curry powder, scotch bonnet pepper, thyme, salt and allspice. Stir again.
3. Add the chicken and the water, stir then cover.
4. Cook on manual high pressure for 6 minutes.
5. Do a natural pressure release for 10 minutes then quick release the rest.
6. Serve and enjoy!

Pakistani Karahi Chicken

This is about as authentic as Pakistani food can get and best of all, it's really easy to make. Who'd have thought that with just a few ingredients you could create food that tastes THIS good??

Cooks: 25 mins
Serves: 6
Net carbs: 4g
Fat: 9g
Protein: 22g

Ingredients:

- 2 Tbsp. oil
- 8 Tbsp. diced or grated ginger
- 1 ½ lb. (680g) boneless skinless chicken thighs cut into 4 pieces each
- 2 cups (400g) canned diced tomatoes
- 1 tsp. ground cumin
- 1 tsp. garam masala
- ½ tsp. cayenne
- 1 tsp. salt

To serve...

- ¼ cup (6g) chopped cilantro or parsley
- 2-3 Tbsp. lemon juice
- 1 tsp. garam masala
- Fresh ginger cut into very thin matchsticks

Method:

1. Open your Instant pot and add the oil.
2. Add the ginger and cook for a few minutes.
3. Throw in the chicken and brown on both sides.
4. Add the tomatoes and spices, stir well then cover.
5. Cook on manual high pressure for 5 minutes.
6. Do a natural pressure release for 10 minutes, then do a quick pressure release.
7. Serve and enjoy!

Easy BBQ Chicken Wings

Want fast, easy BBQ chicken that you can throw into the pot and leave to cook? Then you've found the perfect recipe for you. Enjoy!

Cooks: 30 minutes
Serves: 6
Net carbs: 2g
Fat: 31g
Protein: 29g

Ingredients:
- 4 lb. (1.8kg) chicken wings trimmed of fat and separated (tips discarded)
- 2-3 Tbsp. seasoned salt - like Cajun garlic powder, or any favorite seasoning mix
- ½ cup (120ml) cold water
- 4 Tbsp. low sugar BBQ sauce
- ½ cup (120ml) Frank's Wing Sauce
- 4 Tbsp. melted butter

Method:
1. Place the salt and garlic powder into a bowl and stir to combine.
2. Throw in the chicken wings and toss until completely covered.
3. Place the water into the Instant pot, drop in the trivet then add the chicken.
4. Cook on manual high for 5 minutes.
5. Do a natural pressure release for 10 minutes then do a quick pressure release.
6. Turn your oven onto broil, cover a baking sheet with aluminum foil, spray with oil and add the wings.
7. Pour half of the sauce over the wings, toss well to coat and broil for a further 5-10 minutes.
8. Pop onto a plate, pour over the rest of the sauce and then serve and enjoy!

Beef

Keto Shepherd's Pie

My mom used to make Shepherd's Pie every Friday when we came home from school. It was her specialty and we could taste the love she put into the thing. That's why I was a tiny bit sad when I turned Keto that I couldn't eat her offerings anymore. But I needn't have worried- this cauliflower version is a pretty good replacement.

Cooks: 40 mins
Serves: 12
Net carbs: 4.1g
Fat: 21.2g
Protein: 21.5g

Ingredients:
- 1 head cauliflower
- 4 Tbsp. butter
- 4 oz. (112g) cream cheese
- 1 free-range egg
- 1 cup (125g) Mozzarella cheese
- Salt and Pepper, to taste
- 1 Tbsp. garlic powder
- 2 lb. (900g) ground beef
- 2 cups (250g) chopped carrots (omit if want to lower carbs)
- 2 cups (300g) frozen peas (omit if want to lower carbs)
- 8 oz. (225g) sliced mushrooms
- 1 cup (235ml) beef broth
- Salt and pepper, to taste

Method:
1. Open the Instant pot, add the water then follow with the trivet.
2. Place the cauliflower inside and cook on manual high for five minutes.
3. Do a quick pressure release and transfer the cauliflower to the blender.
4. Add the butter, cream cheese, egg, mozzarella and seasoning into the blender and hit that whizz button.
5. Remove the trivet from the Instant pot and drain the water.

6. Place the ground beef, garlic powder, carrots, peas, mushrooms, beef, salt and pepper into the Instant Pot and mix well.
7. Put the cauliflower mix over the top of the Instant pot, pop the lid back on and cook on manual high for 10 minutes.
8. Do a natural pressure release for 10 minutes then do a quick pressure release.

Butter Beef

Do you adore the taste of roast beef but want to try something different? Cook this one. It's oh-so tender, perfect shredded and enjoyed wrapped in lettuce and yummy whenever you feel like a treat. If the carb count is too high, omit the peppers and replace with smoked paprika or even chili instead.

Serves: 6
Net carbs: 5g
Fat: 32g
Protein: 66g

Ingredients:
- 3 lb. (1.4kg) beef roast
- 1 Tbsp. olive oil
- 2 Tbsp. ranch dressing seasoning mix
- 1 jar pepper rings, drained with 1/4 cup (60ml) of juice reserved
- 2 Tbsp. zesty Italian seasoning mix
- 8 Tbsp. butter
- 1 cup (235ml) water

Method:
1. Start by turning the Instant Pot onto sauté and add the oil.
2. Place the roast into the bottom and brown on all sides. Turn off the Instant pot.
3. Add the water, seasoning, pepper rings and juice, topped by the butter.
4. Cover, and cook on manual high pressure for 60 minutes.
5. Do a quick pressure release then open.
6. Shred the beef.
7. Serve and enjoy!

No Noodle Beef Lasagna

I never thought that a lasagna without pasta would be possible. But it's better than possible- it's BETTER! Awesome flavor, awesome texture...Mmm...I'm getting hungry!

Cooks: 35 mins
Serves: 2
Net carbs: 6g
Fats: 25g
Protein: 25g

Ingredients:

- 1 lb. (450g) ground beef
- 2 cloves garlic
- 1 small onion
- 1 ½ cups (250g) ricotta cheese
- ½ cup (60g) Parmesan cheese
- 1 large free-range egg
- 24 oz. (680g) marinara sauce
- 8 oz. (225g) mozzarella

Method:

1. Open up your Instant pot, add the oil and switch onto sauté.
2. Add the ground beef, onion and garlic and cook until browned.
3. Meanwhile, grab a bowl and combine the ricotta, parmesan and egg.
4. Drain the oil from the pot and remove the meat mixture.
5. Place the meat into a soufflé dish that fits into your Instant pot, pour the sauce over the meat and stir well. Remove 1//2 of the meat mixture and pop to one side.
6. Add the ricotta mixture, then more meat sauce then top with the mozzarella.
7. Add more ricotta then more mozzarella. Sprinkle with freshly ground black pepper and cover with foil.
8. Pour the water into the Instant pot, add the trivet then lower the soufflé dish inside.
9. Cover and cook on manual high pressure for 10 minutes.
10. Do a natural pressure release for 10 minutes then do a quick pressure release.
11. Sprinkle with parmesan then serve and enjoy!

Balsamic Beef

Keto purists might wrinkle their noses at the sheer mention of Balsamic vinegar because the stuff does contain some carbs. But for those of us who like to relax the rules slightly, this recipe is right up our street. Rich, herby and delicious, it's absolutely incredible. And if you do want to lower the carbs, replace with another vinegar but be warned- it won't be the same.

Cooks: 1 hour
Serves: 6
Net carbs: 2.5g
Fat: 34.1g
Protein: 60.1g

Ingredients:
- 3 lb. (1.4 kg) chuck roast
- 3 cloves garlic
- 1 Tbsp. oil
- 1 tsp. salt
- ½ tsp. pepper
- ½ tsp. rosemary
- 1 Tbsp. butter
- ½ tsp. thyme
- 4 Tbsp. balsamic vinegar
- 1 cup (235ml) beef broth

Method:
1. Start by preparing the roast. Slit all over and pop the garlic slices in the wholes.
2. Then place the salt, pepper, rosemary and thyme into a bowl and rub over the meat.
3. Open the Instant pot, turn onto sauté and add the oil.
4. Place the roast into the pot and brown.
5. Remove the meat and add the butter, vinegar and broth. Scrape well to deglaze.
6. Return the roast to the pot and cover.
7. Cook on manual high for 40 minutes.
8. Do a quick pressure release.
9. Serve and enjoy!

Beef Kheema Meatloaf

Meatloaf doesn't have to be boring!! Create this spicy Indian meatloaf in your Instant pot and gasp as how yummy it really is. Wow!

Cooks: 28 mins
Serves: 4
Net carbs: 5g
Fat: 13g
Protein: 26g

Ingredients:
- 1 lb. (450g) ground beef
- 2 free-range eggs
- 1 cup (150g) onion, diced
- ¼ cup (6g) cilantro, chopped
- 1 Tbsp. minced ginger
- 1 Tbsp. minced garlic
- 2 tsp. garam masala
- 1 tsp. salt
- 1 tsp. turmeric
- 1 tsp. cayenne
- ½ tsp. ground cinnamon
- 1/8 tsp. ground cardamom

Method:
1. Take a large bowl and combine all the ingredients.
2. Grease the inside of a loaf tin (that will fit into your Instant Pot) and press the meat mixture into the bottom.
3. Drop into your Instant pot and cover with the lid.
4. Cook on manual high pressure for 20 minutes.
5. Do a quick pressure release.
6. Remove from the Instant pot, rest for 10 minutes then serve and enjoy!

Beef Short Ribs

Mmm...ribs...Need I say any more? Cook them. They're good.

Cooks: 1 hour
Serves: 12
Net carbs: 2g
Fat: 42g
Protein: 16g

Ingredients:

- 4 lb. (1.8kg) boneless or bone in, beef short ribs
- Salt and pepper, to taste
- 2 Tbsp. olive oil
- 1 cup (235ml) beef broth
- 1 ½ cups (225g) onion
- 3 cloves garlic
- 2 Tbsp. Worcestershire sauce (low sugar)
- 2 Tbsp. tomato paste
- 1 ½ cups (355ml) red wine

Method:

1. Start by turning your Instant pot onto sauté and adding the oil.
2. Season the ribs then place into the pot. Cook until brown, then pot to one side.
3. Add the broth to the Instant pot, scrape well then pop the ribs back inside.
4. Add the remaining ingredients then cover and cook on manual high for 25 minutes.
5. Do a natural pressure release for 10 minutes then a quick pressure release.
6. Serve and enjoy!

Mexican Shredded Beef

Wow! Shredded beef with chili is the ultimate treat for a massive chili fan like me. And when you add the liquid smoke, it charges the dish with the best ever flavor that is a great crowd-pleaser.

Cooks: 1 hour 10 minutes
Serves: 12
Net carbs: 1.9g
Fat: 27.8g
Protein: 29.5g

Ingredients:
- 5 lb. (2.2kg) chuck roast
- Salt and pepper, to taste
- 4 Tbsp. olive oil
- 1 x 15 oz. (425g) can diced tomatoes
- 1 cup (235ml) water
- 2 Tbsp. liquid smoke (optional)
- 4 garlic cloves, minced
- 1 tsp. ground cumin
- 1 Tbsp. chili powder

Method:
1. Open the Instant pot and turn onto sauté. Add the oil.
2. Season the roast with salt and pepper and place the roast inside the Instant pot, cooking until brown.
3. Add the tomatoes, water, liquid smoke, garlic, cumin and chipotle powder. Stir well to combine.
4. Cover and cook on manual high for around 60 minutes.
5. Do a natural pressure release for 10 minutes then quick release.
6. Serve and enjoy!

Beef Chili Recipe

This chili is much higher carb than the bean-free version we shared earlier, but it's still delicious and worth adding to the recipe. Lower the carbs include omitting the Worcester sauce. Delicious!

Cooks: 45 minutes
Serves: 10
Net carbs: 7g
Fat: 18g
Protein: 23g

Ingredients:

- 2 ½ lb. (1.1kg) ground beef
- ½ large onion, chopped
- 8 cloves garlic, minced
- 2 x 15 oz. (425g) cans diced tomatoes with liquid
- 1 x 16 oz. (450g) can tomato paste
- 1 x 14 oz. (400g) can green chilis with liquid
- 2 Tbsp. Worcester sauce (low sugar)
- 4 Tbsp. chili powder (or to taste)
- 2 Tbsp. cumin
- 1 Tbsp. dried oregano
- 2 tsp. sea salt
- 1 tsp. black pepper
- 1 bay leaf (opt.)
- 1 cup (235ml) beef broth

Method:

1. Open the Instant pot, add the oil then the onion. Cook for 5 minutes.
2. Add the garlic then the ground beef and cook until browned.
3. Add the remaining ingredients and stir until combined.
4. Cook on manual high for 35 minutes.
5. Do a natural pressure release for 10 minutes then do a quick pressure release.
6. Serve and enjoy!

Fast Italian Meatballs

I thought that meatballs in the Instant Pot would be really complicated to make and taste a bit...well...weird. But these are amazing! You really can throw them together in a few minutes and have them on the table fast. Be sure to double check the carb content on the pre-made sauce though...

Cooks: 30 minutes
Serves: 5
Net carbs: 5g
Fat: 33g
Protein: 34g

Ingredients:
For the meatballs:
- 1 ½ lb. (680g) ground beef
- 2 Tbsp. fresh parsley, chopped
- ¾ cup (90g) grated parmesan cheese
- ½ cup (96g) almond flour
- 2 free-range eggs
- 1 tsp. kosher salt
- ¼ tsp. ground black pepper
- ¼ tsp. garlic powder
- 1 tsp. dried onion flakes
- ¼ tsp. dried oregano
- 1/3 cup (80ml) warm water

To cook the meatballs:
- 1 tsp. olive oil
- 3 cups (705ml) marinara sauce (check that it's sugar-free)

Method:
1. Grab a large bowl and add the meatball ingredients. Stir well until combined.
2. Form into 12-15 balls.
3. Turn the Instant pot onto sauté and add the oil.
4. Place the meatballs into the Instant pot and brown on all sides.
5. Turn off the heat, then pour the marinara sauce over the top.
6. Cook on manual low pressure for 10 minutes.
7. Do a natural pressure release.
8. Serve and enjoy.

Italian Beef with Peppers

The Italians REALLY know how to create the most flavorsome beef on this planet. Know how they do it? They combine fragrant herbs, onions, peppers and a whole lotta love. If the carb content with this one bothers you, omit the peppers and replace with tomatoes, garlic or spices.

Cooks: 1 hour 10 minutes
Serves: 8
Net carbs: 5g
Fat: 3g
Protein: 4g

Ingredients:
- 6 lb. (2.7kg) chuck roast
- 1 Tbsp. canola oil
- 2 Tbsp. Italian dressing seasoning mix
- 1 x 16 oz. (450g) jar sliced pepperochini peppers
- ½ yellow onion, thinly sliced
- 1 cup (235ml) water

Method:
1. Open your Instant pot and turn onto sauté. Add the oil.
2. Place the roast into the Instant pot and cook until brown on all sides.
3. Add the onions, half of the pepperochini pepper, 4 tablespoons of the brine, the Italian seasoning and the water.
4. Cover and cook on manual high pressure for 60 minutes.
5. Do a quick pressure release.
6. Remove the roast and shred then return to the pot.
7. Stir through the remaining peppers.
8. Serve and enjoy!

Cheese Steak Pot Roast

Purists and carnivores are going to go crazy for this one-pot meal. It has everything you could desire when it comes to flavor and it's pretty easy to make too. Enjoy!

Cooks: 2 hours 10 mins
Serves: 8
Net carbs: 3.5g
Fat: 25.7g
Protein: 46.1g

Ingredients:
- 1 Tbsp. oil
- 8 oz. (225g) mushrooms
- 2 large onions
- 2 green peppers
- 1-2 Tbsp. Montreal steak seasoning
- 3 lb. (1.35kg) chuck roast
- 1 Tbsp. butter
- ½ cup beef stock

Method:
1. Open the Instant pot and set to sauté. Add the oil.
2. Place the chuck roast into a large bowl and rub the steak seasoning on all sides.
3. Pop into the Instant pot and cook on all sides until brown. Remove and pop to one side.
4. Add the butter and onions and soften. Scrape whilst cooking to keep that nice stick stuff.
5. Then add the peppers, mushrooms and stock.
6. Cover and cook on manual high for 70 mins.
7. Do a natural pressure release.
8. Serve and enjoy.

Indian Kheema Beef

Not all Indian beef need to be blow-your-head-off kind of spicy! It can also be kid-friendly, easy to create and perfect for a quick mid-week meal.

Cooks: 30 minutes
Serves: 4
Net carbs: 17g
Fat: 13g
Protein: 28g

Ingredients:
- 1 cup (150g) onion, chopped
- 1 Tbsp. minced ginger
- 1 Tbsp. garlic
- 3-4 pieces cinnamon sticks
- 4 pods green or white cardamom
- 1 lb. (450g) ground beef
- 1 tsp. garam masala
- 1 tsp. salt
- ½ tsp. turmeric
- ½ tsp. cayenne pepper (adjust to preferred spice level)
- ½ tsp. ground coriander
- ½ tsp. cumin
- ¼ cup (60ml) water

Method:
1. Open up the Instant pot, turn onto sauté and add the oil.
2. Add the cinnamon and cardamom and leave to cook for 10 seconds.
3. Add the onions, garlic and ginger and cook until translucent.
4. Add the beef, then the remaining spices and stir well.
5. Cover and cook on manual high for 5 minutes.
6. Do a natural pressure release for 10 minutes, then a quick pressure release.
7. Serve and enjoy!

Beef Stroganoff

Hands up if you LOVE Beef Stroganoff...Yeah, me too! This one is beautifully low carb and tastes simply out of this world. Reduce the carb count even more by omitting the Worcester sauce or substituting for a pinch of ginger, mustard powder and cinnamon. Beautiful!

Cooks: 35 mins
Serves: 4
Net carbs: 9g
Fat: 16g
Protein: 33g

Ingredients:
- 1 Tbsp. oil
- ½ cup (75g) diced onions
- 1 Tbsp. garlic
- 1 lb. (450g) pork tips or beef stew meat
- 1 ½ cups (110g) chopped mushrooms
- 1 Tbsp. Worcestershire sauce (choose low-sugar)
- 1 tsp. salt
- ½ tsp. pepper
- ¾ cup (180ml) water

To serve...
- 1/3 cup (85g) sour cream
- ¼ tsp. xanthan gum

Method:
1. Open the Instant pot and turn onto sauté. Add the oil.
2. Add onions and garlic and cook until soft.
3. Add the remaining ingredients except for the sour cream and cover.
4. Cook on manual high pressure for 20 minutes.
5. Do a natural pressure release.
6. Open and turn back onto sauté.
7. Stir through the sour cream.
8. Sprinkle the xanthan gum over the top and stir until thickens.
9. Serve and enjoy!

Pork

Mexican Pulled Pork

Oh wow! Pulled pork is another of my favorite dishes on the whole planet. (And yes, you will hear me say that a lot during this book. I'm a foodie, what can I say?) It's super simple to make and tastes amazing whatever you choose to use it for. Even on its own, it's stunningly tasty.

Cooks: 1 hour 15 mins
Serves: 6
Net carbs: 2g
Fats: 4g
Protein: 25g

Ingredients:
- 1 Tbsp. Splenda
- 1 tsp. garlic powder
- 1 tsp. onion powder
- 1 tsp. smoked paprika
- 1 tsp. ground cumin
- 1 tsp. salt
- ½ tsp. Ancho chili powder
- ½ tsp. black pepper
- 1 ½ lb. (680g) boneless pork shoulder, cut into 5
- ¼ cup (60ml) water

Method:
1. Take a large bowl and add the sweetener, garlic powder, onion, paprika, salt, chili and black pepper.
2. Add the pork shoulder and rub the spice into the meat. Leave for around an hour to marinade.
3. Open up the Instant pot, add the trivet and the water.
4. Place the pork inside and cover.
5. Cook on manual high for 25 minutes.
6. Do a natural pressure release for 10 minutes then a quick pressure release.
7. Remove the pork and shred.
8. Serve and enjoy!

Pork Short Ribs

All you need to make these ribs is a couple of basic ingredients and you'll create an epic meal that you just can't help but devour. There's no time to waste- make them now!

Cooks: 30 mins
Serves: 6
Net carbs: 1g
Fat: 16g
Protein: 19g

Ingredients:
- 2 lb. (900g) beef short ribs, bone-in
- Salt and pepper, to taste
- 2 Tbsp. olive oil
- ½ cup (120ml) dry red wine
- 3 cloves garlic, sliced

Method:
1. Place the ribs onto a flat surface and season well with salt and pepper.
2. Open the Instant pot, turn onto sauté and add the oil.
3. Cook the ribs until brown on all sides.
4. Return the meat to the pot and add the wine, garlic and a touch of extra seasoning. Stir well.
5. Cover and cook on manual high for 50 minutes.
6. Do a natural pressure release.
7. Serve and enjoy!

Pork Chile Verde

This recipe boasts a delicious homemade chili sauce complete with roasted garlic, my favorite herb ever- cilantro and sooo much flavor. You'll notice that I ask you to do a natural pressure release- try to do this if you have the time. It will be worth the wait!

Cooks: 1 hour
Serves: 12
Net carbs: 4g
Fat: 8g
Protein: 24g

Ingredients:

- 1 bulb of garlic, the bottom sliced off
- 2 Tbsp. + 1 tsp. olive oil, divided
- 2 lb. (900g) tomatillos, husks removed (can sub with unripe tomatoes and a squeeze of lime)
- 1 green bell pepper, roughly chopped
- 1 yellow onion, peeled and quartered
- 2-3 green chilies, roasted
- 1 bunch cilantro, divided
- Salt & pepper, to taste
- 3 lb. (1.4kg) pork shoulder or picnic roast, cubed
- 1 tsp. cumin
- 2 tsp. oregano
- 2 bay leaves
- 1 cup (235ml) chicken broth

Method:

1. Open up the Instant pot, add the oil and place the pepper, onion, tomatillo and garlic on the bottom.
2. Cover and cook on manual high pressure for 10 minutes. Do a quick pressure release.
3. Open up and remove the head of garlic. Carefully squeeze from the skin and into a blender.
4. Add the remaining ingredients into the blender with the cilantro and chilis.
5. Clean the inside of your Instant pot and add the remaining oil.

6. Throw in the pork and add the salt and pepper, cumin and oregano. Cook until browned.
7. Add the bay leaves, pour the sauce over the top and add the chicken broth. Stir well.
8. Cover and cook on manual high pressure for 30 minutes.
9. Do a natural pressure release.
10. Serve and enjoy!

Smothered Pork Chops

Imagine succulent pork chops, surrounded by beautiful baby mushrooms, a creamy sauce and spiced with onion, garlic, cayenne, and paprika...Sounds dreamily good, right?

Cooks: 45 mins
Serves: 4
Net carbs: 4g
Fat: 32g
Protein: 39g

Ingredients:

- 4 x 6 oz. (170g) boneless pork loin chops
- 1 Tbsp. paprika
- 1 tsp. garlic powder
- 1 tsp. onion powder
- 1 tsp. black pepper
- 1 tsp. salt
- ¼ tsp. cayenne pepper
- 2 Tbsp. coconut oil
- ½ medium onion, sliced
- 6 oz. (170g) sliced baby Bella mushrooms
- 1 Tbsp. butter
- ½ cup (120ml) heavy cream
- ¼ - ½ tsp. xanthan gum
- 1 Tbsp. chopped fresh parsley

Method:

1. Start by combining the paprika, garlic, onion powder, black pepper, salt and cayenne in a bowl.
2. Place the pork chops into the mixture and rub the spice mixture well into the meat.
3. Open the Instant pot, turn onto sauté and add the oil.
4. Place the chops into the Instant pot and cook until brown. Remove and pop onto a plate.
5. Add the onions and mushrooms to the Instant pot, stir well then return the chops to the pan.
6. Cover and cook on manual high for 25 minutes.

7. Do a natural pressure release and remove the pork. Place onto a serving plate.
8. Turn the Instant pot back onto sauté and add the butter, cream and remaining spices. Stir well.
9. Sprinkle the xanthan gum over the liquid and stir until thick.
10. Serve and enjoy!

Korean Spicy Pork

The Koreans really know how to dress their pork, especially with dishes like this. The balance of flavors is simply amazing: it's salty, it's spicy, it's sweet and it's melt-in-the-mouth good. Wow! Reduce the carbs by switching the red chili paste for power and watching out for added sugars.

Cooks: 40mins
Serves: 4
Net carbs: 6g
Fat: 9g
Protein: 15g

Ingredients:

- 1 lb. (450g) pork shoulder, cut into slices
- 1 onion, thinly sliced
- 1 Tbsp. minced ginger
- 1 Tbsp. minced garlic
- 1 Tbsp. soy sauce
- 1 Tbsp. rice wine
- 1 Tbsp. sesame oil
- 2 packets Splenda
- 2 Tbsp. gochujang (red chili paste)
- ¼ tsp. cayenne pepper
- ¼ cup (60ml) water

To serve...

- 1 onion sliced thinly
- 1 Tbsp. sesame seeds
- 4 Tbsp. sliced green onions

Method:

1. Place all the ingredients into the Instant pot and stir well. Leave to rest for an hour.
2. Cover and cook on manual high pressure for 20 minutes.
3. Do a natural pressure release for 10 minutes then do a quick pressure release.
4. Open the pot.
5. Heat a heavy pan over the stove.
6. Add the pork, the green onion and 4-6 tablespoons of the sauce. The sauce will start to caramelize and thicken.
7. Stir well until most of the sauce has disappeared.
8. Sprinkle with sesame seeds then serve and enjoy.

Spicy Cajun Pork & Spinach Feast

Use what you have in your pantry and freezer and create the perfect last-minute meal. It tastes wonderful and provides plenty of energy-friendly vitamins and minerals too.

Cooks: 40mins
Serves: 4
Net Carbs: 7g
Fat: 17g
Protein: 23g

Ingredients:

- 1 large onion
- 4 cloves garlic
- 10 oz. (280g) canned tomatoes with chili
- 1 tsp. dried thyme
- 2 tsp. Cajun seasoning blend
- 1 lb. (450g) pork butt, cut into chunks

To serve...

- ½ cup (120ml) heavy whipping cream
- 4 cups (900g) chopped baby spinach

Method:

1. Place the onion, garlic and canned tomatoes into the blender and whizz until smooth.
2. Pour into your Instant pot and add the Cajun seasoning. Stir well.
3. Add the pork cubes and stir again.
4. Cook on manual high pressure for 20 minutes.
5. Do a natural pressure release for 10 minutes, then a quick pressure release.
6. Turn the Instant pot onto sauté and stir through the cream.
7. Add the spinach, warm until the spinach wilts then serve and enjoy!

Ginger Pork Tenderloin

Grab yourself the spices, stir then up and then bathe your pork in the flavors before cooking and tucking in. Meals couldn't be simpler.

Cooks: 45 minutes (plus at least one hour to marinate)
Serves: 4
Net carbs: 0g
Fat: 5g
Protein: 10g

Ingredients:

- ½ cups (120ml) soy sauce
- 1 Tbsp. fresh ginger, peeled and diced
- 1 tsp. sweetener
- 2 Tbsp. lemon juice
- ½ cups (25g) chopped cilantro
- 2 tsp. garlic, minced
- 1 ½ lb. (680g) quarter pork tenderloin

Method:

1. Place the soy sauce, ginger, sweetener and lemon juice into a bowl. Stir well.
2. Add the cilantro and garlic and stir again.
3. Add the pork, stir well and leave to marinate for at least an hour.
4. Transfer to your Instant pot then cover.
5. Cook on manual high for 30 minutes.
6. Do a natural pressure release for 10 minutes then do a quick pressure release.
7. Serve and enjoy.

Creamy Parmesan Garlic Pork Chops

Bring on the cheese! If you're a fan of the tangy stuff and you want to sample pork chops with a difference, put this on the list for dinner tonight. They're fast, yummy and oh-so satisfying.

Cooks: 45 minutes
Serves: 6
Net carbs: 2.5g
Fat: 36.5g
Protein: 48.9g protein

Ingredients:
- 1 ½ lb. (680g) boneless pork chops
- ½ medium onion, sliced
- 2 garlic cloves, minced
- 2 Tbsp. olive oil
- 1 cup (240ml) heavy whipping cream
- 1 oz. (22.5g) cream cheese
- 1/3 cup (80ml) chicken broth
- 1/3 cup (80g) parmesan cheese
- 1/2 cup (80g) cheddar cheese
- 1 Tbsp. Italian seasoning
- ½ tsp. pepper
- Salt to taste

Method:
1. Open the Instant pot and set to sauté. Add the oil.
2. Place the onion, garlic and pork chops inside and stir well.
3. Cook until browned, then remove the pork and place to one side.
4. Add the remaining ingredients to the pot then stir well.
5. Return the pork to the pan and cover.
6. Cook on manual high for 30 minutes.
7. Do a natural pressure release for 10 minutes then a quick pressure release for 5 minutes.
8. Serve and enjoy!

Cheesy Pork with Noodles

Shirataki noodle are light and fine noodles made from yam. They're much lower carb than other noodles and they are AMAZING!

Cooks: 20 mins
Serves: 6
Net carbs: 3g
Fat: 18g
Protein: 15g

Ingredients:
- 1 Tbsp. oil
- 1 lb. (450g) ground pork
- ½ cup (75g) chopped onion
- 2 cloves garlic
- 1 cup (175g) chopped bell peppers
- 4 cups (900g) chopped baby spinach
- ½ cup (60g) grated parmesan cheese
- 2 packages shirataki noodles

Method:
1. Open up your Instant pot, turn onto sauté and add the oil.
2. Add the ground pork and cook until pork is changing color.
3. Add the onion and garlic, stirring well and scraping the pan.
4. Add the pepper and the spinach and cover with the lid.
5. Cook on manual high pressure for 5 minutes.
6. Do a quick pressure release.
7. Serve and enjoy!

Buttery Pork Chops

Simple, tasty, melt-in-the-mouth. Amazing.

Cooks: 10 mins
Serves: 5
Net Carbs: 0g
Fat: 22g
Protein: 3g

Ingredients:
- 1 Tbsp. coconut oil
- 4-6 boneless pork chops
- 4 oz. (110g) butter
- 2 Tbsp. Ranch mix
- 1 cup (235ml) water

Method:
1. Open up the Instant pot, turn onto sauté and add the oil.
2. Place the pork into the Instant pot and cook until browned on all sides. Turn off the heat.
3. Next add a small amount of the butter onto each and top with the ranch mix.
4. Pour the water over everything, then cover with the lid.
5. Cook on manual high pressure for five minutes.
6. Do a natural pressure release for 5 minutes and then a quick pressure release.
7. Serve and enjoy!

Lamb

Kashmiri Lamb Rogan Josh

I always think it's sad that lamb isn't more popular because it can be so deliciously tender, juicy and ultra-yummy when it has been cooked in an Instant pot. This recipe does lamb proud. Try it!

Cooks: 45 mins
Serves: 4
Net carbs: 5g
Fat: 3g
Protein: 16g

Ingredients:
- 1 lb. (450g) leg of lamb, cut into cubes
- 1 red onion, diced
- 4 cloves garlic, minced
- 2 tsp. minced ginger minced
- ¼ cup (60g) Greek yogurt
- 1 Tbsp. tomato paste
- 4 Tbsp. cilantro, chopped
- 2 tsp. garam masala
- 1 tsp. smoked paprika
- 1-2 tsp. salt
- 1 tsp. turmeric
- ½ tsp. ground cinnamon
- ¼ - 1 tsp. cayenne pepper (adjust to your taste)

Method:
1. Place all the ingredients into your Instant pot and stir.
2. Leave to marinade for an hour or so (if you have time).
3. Cover and cook on manual high for 20 minutes.
4. Do a natural pressure release for 10 minutes then a quick pressure release.
5. Serve and enjoy!

Greek Lamb Gyros

Imagine making a meatloaf that's packed with fragrant herbs, onion and garlic, then seasoned lightly and cooked to perfection. THAT'S what you get with this Greek Lamb Gyros dish. Serve on its own, served with freshly steamed kale drizzled with olive oil or even eat the leftovers cold from the fridge the next day. Whatever works, right?

Cooks: 45mins
Serves: 4
Net carbs: 13g
Fat: 7g
Protein: 23g

Ingredients:

- 2 lb. (900g) ground lamb
- 5 oz. (140g) onion
- 8 cloves garlic, chopped
- 2 tsp. ground marjoram
- 2 tsp. dried rosemary
- 2 tsp. dried oregano
- 2 tsp. salt
- ¼ tsp. black pepper

To Serve...

- 2 cups Tzatziki sauce recipe, feta cheese, chopped fresh tomatoes, thinly sliced onions Greek Pitta, lettuce, cucumber

Method:

1. Place the onions, garlic, marjoram, rosemary, oregano, and salt and pepper. Whizz until finely chopped.
2. Next add the lamb and whizz again.
3. Grab a loaf tin that will fit into your Instant pot, grease and press the meat mixture into the bottom.
4. Cover with the foil and poke a few steam holes into the top.
5. Add the water to the bottom of your Instant pot, add the trivet and place the pan inside.
6. Cover and cook on manual high pressure for 15 minutes.
7. Do a natural pressure release.
8. Remove the pan from the Instant pot and leave to rest for a further 15 minutes.
9. Slice thinly and enjoy!

Lamb Korma Curry

Don't be deterred from making this delicious lamb korma by looking at the list of spices. You just need to throw them in and forget about them until they're smelling amazing and you have the best, creamiest, most mouthwatering curry you have ever imagined. Wow!

Cooks: 15 mins
Serves: 4
Net carbs: 4g
Fat: 18g
Protein: 23g

Ingredients:

- 1 lb. (450g) lamb leg steak, cut into pieces
- 1 Tbsp. olive oil
- 1 medium onion, chopped
- 2 Tbsp. ginger-garlic paste
- 2 Tbsp. tomato paste
- ½ cup (120ml) coconut milk
- ¼ cup (60ml) + ½ cup (120ml) water (added in two steps)
- Salt, to taste
- 3 tsp. Garam Masala
- ½ tsp. turmeric powder
- ¼ tsp. cayenne pepper
- 1 tsp. paprika
- ½ tsp. cardamom powder

To serve...
- 2 Tbsp. fresh chopped cilantro, for garnish
- ½ - 1 tsp. fresh lime juice before serving (optional)

Method:

1. Open up the Instant pot and turn onto sauté mode. Add the oil.
2. Add the onions and garlic-ginger paste and cook for a minute.
3. Next add the tomato paste and the ¼ cup of water. Stir well.
4. Follow this with the coconut milk, remaining water and lamb.
5. Cover and cook on manual high pressure for 15 minutes.
6. Do a natural pressure release for 15 minutes then do a quick pressure release.
7. Serve and enjoy!

Leg of Lamb with Gravy

When Sunday rolls around and you want to create a delicious roast meat for the family, you don't want to be spending all your time slaving away in your kitchen. You just want to prepare it, cook it, then tuck in. That's exactly what you can do with this super-easy leg of lamb. Enjoy!

Cooks: 2 hours
Serves: 4
Net carbs: 4.5g
Fat: 15g
Protein: 25g

Ingredients:
For the lamb...
- 4 lb. (1.8kg) boneless leg of lamb
- 1 ½ cups (360ml) water
- ½ cup (120ml) white wine
- 2 Tbsp. olive oil
- 1 tsp. dried thyme or oregano
- 1 tsp. garlic powder
- Chopped fresh parsley
- Salt and pepper, to taste

For the gravy...
- 3 Tbsp. salted butter
- 2 Tbsp. Xanthan gum
- Salt and pepper, to taste

Method:
1. Place the lamb onto a flat surface and cover with salt, pepper, garlic and thyme. Pat well to coat.
2. Open up the Instant pot, turn to sauté and add one tablespoon of the oil.
3. Add the lamb to the pot and brown. Remove and place onto a plate.
4. Add the wine to the pot and turn off.
5. Add the water then stir well.
6. Add the lamb, cover and cook on manual high for 90 minutes.
7. Do a natural pressure release for 20 minutes.
8. Remove the lamb, place onto a baking sheet and drizzle with the remaining oil.
9. Place into a preheated oven for 15 minutes to crisp up. (This last step is very much worth the effort!)
10. Serve and enjoy!

Seafood

Brazilian Fish Stew

In my opinion, NOTHING beats the taste of white fish marinated in lime juice, especially if it comes with a garlic-chili-coconut-coriander sauce. Especially if it's ready faster than you can say Copacabana...well...almost.

Cooks: 50 mins
Serves: 6
Net carbs: 4g
Fat: 29g
Protein: 37g

Ingredients:
- 2 ¼ lb. (1 kg) white fish
- 2 limes, juiced
- Salt, to taste
- 2 Tbsp. vegetable oil
- 1 onion
- 2 bell peppers (green)
- 2 garlic cloves
- 1 red chili
- 2 cups (480ml) fish stock
- 14 oz. (400g) tin chopped tomatoes
- 1 cup (240ml) coconut milk
- 1 tsp. minced cilantro

Method:
1. Start by placing the fish into a ceramic bowl, adding the lime juice and a touch of salt.
2. Mix well and place into the fridge for 30 minutes.
3. Open up the Instant pot and add the oil, followed by the onion.
4. Add the peppers, garlic and chili and cook for 5 minutes more.
5. Add the stock, tomatoes, coconut milk, palm oil and coriander, stirring well.
6. Add the fish and the marinade.
7. Cover with the lid and cook on manual low pressure for 2 minutes.
8. Do a natural pressure release.
9. Serve and enjoy!

Shrimp with Tomatoes and Feta

If I'm honest, this incredible combination of shrimp, tomatoes and feta never manages to feed six in my house because I just can't help going back for more. And more. And more. It's addictive stuff- be warned!

Cooks: 25 mins
Serves: 6
Net carbs: 5g
Fat: 11g
Protein: 19g

Ingredients:
- 2 Tbsp. butter
- 1 Tbsp. garlic puree
- ½ tsp. red pepper flakes
- 1 ½ cups chopped onion
- 1 x 14.5 oz. (410g) can tomatoes
- 1 tsp. oregano
- 1 tsp. salt
- 1 lb. (450g) frozen shrimp 21-25 count, shelled

To serve...
- 1 cup (150g) crumbled feta cheese
- ½ cup (65g) sliced black olives
- ¼ cup (6g) parsley

Method:
1. Open up the Instant pot, turn onto sauté and add the butter.
2. Then add the garlic, onion, red pepper flakes, tomato, oregano and salt. Stir well.
3. Add the shrimp then stir again and cover.
4. Cook on manual low pressure for one minute.
5. Do a quick pressure release then stir well.
6. Sprinkle over the feta, olives and parsley and serve.
7. Enjoy!

Chinese Style Steamed Ginger Scallion Fish

Create this light, Chinese-style fish dish and you'll have dinner ready in the blink of an eye and be licking your lips when it's all done. Amazing.

Cooks: 20 mins
Serves: 4
Net carbs: 4g
Fats: 5g
Protein: 24g

Ingredients:

- 3 Tbsp. soy sauce
- 2 Tbsp. rice wine
- 1 Tbsp. Chinese black bean paste (check for hidden sugars)
- 1 tsp. minced ginger
- 1 tsp. garlic
- 1 lb. (450g) firm white fish such as tilapia
- 1 Tbsp. peanut oil
- 2 Tbsp. julienned ginger
- ¼ cup (40g) green onions/scallions
- ¼ cup (6g) chopped cilantro
- 2 cups (470ml) water

Method:

1. Place the fish into a ceramic bowl.
2. Combine the soy sauce, rice wine, black bean paste, and garlic in a bowl and pour over the fish.
3. Leave to rest in the fridge for at least an hour.
4. Place the water into your Instant pot and drop in the steamer.
5. Remove the fish from the marinade and place into your Instant pot (but keep that marinade!)
6. Cover and cook on manual low pressure for 2 minutes.
7. Do a quick pressure release.
8. Pop a skillet over a heat, add the oil and cook the ginger, scallions and cilantro.
9. Add the reserved marinate, stir well and bring to the boil.
10. Pour over the fish, then enjoy!

Easy Shrimp with Coconut Milk

If those rich, heavy curries really aren't your thing, and you've given up on ever loving the spicy stuff, give these easy shrimp a go. Swimming in coconut milk and delicately flavored with ginger, garlic, cayenne and garam masala, you might find yourself a convert too!

Cooks: 10 minutes
Serves: 4
Net carbs: 3g
Fat: 12g
Protein: 16g

Ingredients:

- 1 lb. (450g) shrimp shelled, deveined (about 26-30 count to the pound)
- 1 Tbsp. minced ginger minced
- 1 Tbsp. garlic minced
- ½ tsp. turmeric
- 1 tsp. salt
- ½ tsp. cayenne pepper
- 1 tsp. garam masala
- 1 cup (235ml) unsweetened coconut milk
- 2 cups (470ml) water

Method:

1. Take a bowl and combine the coconut milk, garam masala, cayenne pepper, salt, turmeric, garlic, and ginger. Stir well.
2. Open the Instant pot, add the water and place the trivet inside.
3. Take a pot that fits into the Instant pot and add the shrimp and coconut mixture.
4. Cover with foil then replace the lid.
5. Cook on manual low pressure for 4 minutes.
6. Do a quick pressure release.
7. Serve and enjoy!

Steamed Fish Patra Ni Maachi

I bet you're an adventurous, forward thinking type. And I'll bet you'd love to find something very unique (at least in the Western world) that will impress your friends and family and that will taste pretty good too. If so, this recipe needs to be your go-to.

Cooks: 15 minutes
Serves: 4
Net carbs: 1g
Fat: 3g
Protein: 22g

Ingredients:
- 1 lb. (450g) tilapia filets (or use other firm, white, mild fish, probably 2 large filets)
- ½ cup (120g) green chutney (no sugar)
- 1 ½ cup (355ml) water

Method:
1. Start by preparing the tilapia. If the fillets are large, cut in half, cover with the green chutney then wrap in parchment paper.
2. Wrap the parchment packet in foil.
3. Place the water into the Instant pot, add the trivet and place the fish inside.
4. Cover and cook on manual low pressure for 2 minutes.
5. Do a quick pressure release.
6. Unfold each packet carefully, being careful of the steam that will escape.
7. Serve and enjoy!

Salmon with Orange Ginger Sauce

Whenever I think about salmon, I remember my grandmother who would only ever cook the stuff on special occasions. And she'd be pretty impressed with this recipe. At first glance, you'd think it doesn't work, but it's every bit as amazing as you might hope.

Cooks: 35 mins
Serves: 4
Net carbs: 1g
Fat: 7g
Protein: 23g

Ingredients:
- 1 lb. (450g) salmon
- 1 Tbsp. dark soy sauce
- 2 tsp. minced ginger
- 1 tsp. minced garlic
- ½ tsp. salt
- 1 tsp. ground pepper
- 2 Tbsp. zero sugar marmalade
- 2 cups (470ml) water

Method:
1. Take a zip lock back and place the sauce ingredients inside. Mix well.
2. Add the salmon and leave to marinate for 15-30 minutes.
3. Open the Instant pot, add the water then drop in the steamer rack.
4. Add the salmon and sauce then cover.
5. Cook for 3 minutes on low pressure.
6. Do a quick pressure release.
7. Serve and enjoy!

Coconut Fish Curry

Listen up you fish curry lovers out there! You NEED to try this recipe. Including plenty of individual spices to create a unique and authentic flavor, your taste buds will feel like they've taken a little dance when this passes your lips.

Cooks: 45 minutes
Serves: 4
Net carbs: 8g
Fat: 18g
Protein: 22g

Ingredients:
- 1 lb. (450g) Tilapia filets, cut into pieces
- 1 Tbsp. olive oil
- ½ tsp. mustard seeds
- 1 x 14 oz. (400ml) coconut milk
- 1 Tbsp. ginger-garlic paste
- 10-15 curry leaves
- ½ medium onion, sliced
- ½ green pepper, sliced
- ½ orange or yellow pepper, sliced
- 1 tsp. salt
- ½ tsp. turmeric
- ½ tsp. red chili powder (adjust to your taste)
- 2 tsp. ground coriander
- 1 tsp. ground cumin
- ½ - 1 tsp. garam masala
- 2-3 sprigs cilantro

To serve...
- ½ tsp. lime juice

Method:
1. Open up the Instant pot and turn onto sauté.
2. Add the oil and the mustard seeds. When the seeds start to move around a bit, add the curry leaves and the ginger-garlic paste.
3. Cook for 30 seconds, then add the onion and peppers.
4. Add the remaining ingredients, stir well then add the coconut milk.

5. Bring to the boil, then add the tilapia.
6. Cover and cook on manual high pressure for 3 minutes.
7. Do a quick pressure release then serve and enjoy!

Hearty Fish Chowder Recipe

Not all fish dishes need to be light and fragrant, because this one is about as hearty as they get! Boasting lashings of rich cream, wonderfully fragrant thyme, and plenty of bacon and radish, your attitude will DEFINTELY be satisfied about a bowl (or several!) of this.

Cooks: 15 minutes

Serves: 6

Net carbs: 3.4g

Fat: 4g

Protein: 23g

Ingredients:

- 4 slices bacon, chopped
- 1 medium onion, chopped
- 3 cups (350g) chopped daikon radish
- 2 ½ cups (600ml) chicken stock
- ½ tsp. dried thyme
- Salt and pepper, to taste
- 2 cups (480ml) heavy cream
- 1 lb. (450g) fresh white fish like cod, pollock or tilapia, chopped

Method:

1. Open the Instant pot, turn onto sauté and add the oil.
2. Cook the bacon until crispy then remove and pop to one side.
3. Add extra oil as needed then the onion and radish. Cook for 10 minutes.
4. Stir through the thyme, salt and pepper, then add the cream and fish, and stir again.
5. Cover and cook on manual low pressure for 2 minutes.
6. Do a quick pressure release, then serve and enjoy!

Lemon-Dill Salmon & Asparagus

Classic lemon and dill salmon served on a bed of fresh asparagus and ready in no time at all? Words are not enough...

Cooks: 10 mins
Serves: 4
Net carbs: 5g
Fat: 4g
Protein: 25g

Ingredients:

- 1 cup (235ml) water
- 3 large sprigs fresh dill (or parsley, basil, thyme, or tarragon)
- 1 clove garlic, crushed
- 1 lb. skin-on salmon
- 1 Tbsp. + 2 Tbsp. butter
- ¾ tsp. + ¼ tsp. sea salt
- 1 tsp. dried garlic
- ½ tsp. dried dill (or parsley, basil, thyme, or tarragon)
- 7 lemon slices, thinly sliced
- 1 small bunch asparagus

Method:

1. Open the Instant pot and pour the water inside. Drop the trivet inside too.
2. Place the salmon onto the trivet, with the skin pointing down.
3. Place a tablespoon of butter onto the salmon, cover with the salt, garlic and dill then top with lemon.
4. Cover the pot then cook on low manual pressure for 4 minutes.
5. Do a quick pressure release.
6. Remove the salmon carefully and throw away the cooking liquid.
7. Place the remaining fat into the Instant pot, add the asparagus, and cook for 4-5 minutes.
8. Serve with the salmon. Enjoy!

Salmon with Chili-Lime Sauce

This super-spicy salmon recipe is right up my street! It's hot, it's soo warming, it's rich and it's exactly what I want to eat every Friday night for the rest of my life. I mean it!

Cooks: 15 mins
Serves: 2
Net carbs: 5g
Fat: 25g
Protein: 29g

Ingredients:

For the salmon:

- 2 salmon fillets
- 1 cup (235ml) water
- Salt and pepper, to taste

For the chili-lime sauce:

- 1 jalapeno
- 1 lime
- 2 cloves garlic
- 1 tsp. sweetener (or to taste)
- 1 Tbsp. olive oil
- 1 Tbsp. hot water
- 1 Tbsp. chopped fresh parsley
- ½ tsp. paprika
- ½ tsp. cumin

Method:

1. Place the sauce ingredients into a bowl, stir to combine and pop to one side
2. Open your Instant pot and add the water. Drop the trivet inside.
3. Place the salmon onto the rack, season with salt and pepper then cover.
4. Cook on manual high pressure for 5 minutes.
5. Do a quick pressure release.
6. Open and pop the salmon onto a serving plate. Drizzle with the sauce and enjoy!

Vegan/Vegetarian & Egg

Vegetarian Butter "Chicken" with Soy Curls

Who says that the meat eaters need to have all the fun? Veggies and vegans can enjoy this incredible butter chicken recipe straight from the Instant pot and still experience the Keto lifestyle.

Cooks: 15 mins
Serves: 6
Net carbs: 6g
Fat: 24g
Protein: 5g

Ingredients:

- 1 x 14.5 oz. (410g) can diced tomatoes
- 5-6 cloves garlic
- 1-2 tsp. minced ginger
- 1 tsp. turmeric
- ½ tsp. cayenne pepper
- 1 tsp. paprika
- 1 tsp. salt
- 1 tsp. garam masala
- 1 tsp. ground cumin
- 1 ½ cups (60g) dry Soy Curls
- 1 cup (235ml) water

To serve:

- 4 oz. (25g) butter, cubed
- 4 oz. (25ml) heavy cream
- 1 tsp. garam masala
- ½ cup (10g) chopped cilantro

Method:

1. Open the Instant pot, add the tomatoes, soy, water and spices and stir to combine.
2. Cover then cook on manual high pressure for 10 minutes.
3. Do a quick pressure release.
4. Pour everything into a clean bowl, cover and set to one side.

5. Next add the butter to your Instant pot and set onto sauté. Add the remaining garam masala and cilantro. Cook for 30 seconds.
6. Add the cream and stir well.
7. Add the tomato and soy back into your pot, stir well and heat until warm again.
8. Serve and enjoy!

Korean Bibimbap

Wow! Who needs meat when you can eat tempeh that tastes like this. Yes, it might be slightly higher carb than most Keto recipes, but it's well-worth enjoying as a treat. If you want to, omit the cauliflower.

Cooks: 25 minutes
Serves: 2
Net carbs: 10g
Fats: 15g
Protein: 20g

Ingredients:
- 1 Tbsp. soy sauce
- 2 Tbsp. rice vinegar (or regular white vinegar)
- 7 oz. (200 g) tempeh, sliced into squares
- 1 Tbsp. + 1 Tbsp. olive oil (divided)
- 4-6 broccoli florets, in thin spears
- ½ cucumber, in strips
- 10 oz. (300 g) raw cauliflower, riced
- 2 Tbsp. gochujang chili paste (no-sugar)
- 2 Tbsp. rice vinegar
- 1 Tbsp. soy sauce
- 1 tsp. sesame oil
- 2 Tbsp. sesame seeds
- Xylitol, to taste

Method:
1. Take a bowl and combine the soy sauce and vinegar.
2. Dip the tempeh squares into the liquid and pop to one side whilst you prep the veggies.
3. Open your Instant pot, pop onto sauté mode, add 1 tablespoon of the oil and pop the tempeh inside. Cook.
4. Next add the other veggies and cook until beginning to soften.
5. Grab a separate pan, add the rest of the oil and cook the cauliflower rice.
6. Mix the chili paste, sesame oil, marinade, and a touch of sweetener. Add oil if required.
7. Place the cauliflower onto a place, add the tempeh and veggies, pour the chili sauce over the top and sprinkle over the sesame seeds.
8. Serve and enjoy!

Korean Style Steamed Eggs

You've gotta love those Korean-style eggs. They're pretty simple but they really tick the protein box for those moments when you have veggies at home, or you're looking for eggs with a different.

Cooks: 10 minutes
Serves: 3
Net carbs: 0g
Fat: 5g
Protein: 6g

Ingredients:
- 3 free-range eggs
- 1 cup (235ml) cold water
- 3 tsp. scallions/ green onions, chopped
- 1 tsp. sesame seeds
- ¼ tsp. garlic powder

Method:
1. Grab a small bowl and mix the eggs and water.
2. Strain and pour into a heatproof bowl.
3. Add the remaining ingredients and mix again.
4. Open your Instant pot, add the cup of water and place the trivet inside.
5. Drop the bowl with the egg mixture into the bottom and cover.
6. Cook on manual high for 5 minutes.
7. Do a quick pressure release.
8. Serve and enjoy!

Eggs de Provence

Mmm...these eggs are pretty darn good, even if I say so myself. Great nutritionally-balanced meal for the whole family, whether you're looking for an eggy-snack or you have a veggie in the house (just leave out the ham or bacon.).

Cooks: 20 mins
Serves: 6
Net carbs: 0g
Fats: 5g
Protein: 6g

Ingredients:
- 6 free-range eggs
- 1 small onion, chopped
- 1 cup (150g) cooked ham or bacon
- ½ cup (120ml) heavy cream
- 1 cup (65g) chopped kale leaves
- 1 cup (125g) Cheddar cheese
- 1 tsp. Herbes de Provence
- Salt and pepper, to taste
- 1 cup (235ml) water

Method:
1. Whisk the eggs in a bowl with the heavy cream.
2. Add the remaining ingredients and mix well.
3. Take a large heat proof dish (that will fit into your Instant pot).
4. Pour the water into the bottom of your Instant pot, drop in the trivet, add the heat proof dish that contains the eggs, then cover.
5. Cook on manual high for 20 minutes.
6. Do a natural pressure release.
7. Serve and enjoy!

Devilled Egg Salad

I love making this egg salad whenever we're heading on a picnic in the summer! It's much more exciting that a regular egg salad, it transports well, and it works brilliantly as a wrap filling when you hunger strikes.

Cooks: 20 minutes
Serves: 5
Net carbs: 1g
Fat: 26g
Protein: 16g

Ingredients:
- 10 free-range eggs
- 5 strips raw bacon
- 2 Tbsp. sugar-free mayonnaise
- 1 tsp. Dijon mustard
- ¼ tsp. smoked paprika
- 1 stalk scallions/green onion
- Salt and pepper, to taste
- 1 cup (235ml) water

Method:
1. Find a large pan (that will fit into your Instant pot) and grease well.
2. Break the eggs into the pan and give them a quick whisk.
3. Pour the water into the bottom of your Instant pot, drop in the trivet and place the pan inside.
4. Cover and cook on manual high pressure for 6 minutes.
5. Do a natural pressure release for 10 minutes.
6. Remove the egg mixture from the pan, tip into a bowl and chop well.
7. Pour away the water from the Instant pot.
8. Set the Instant pot onto sauté and add the olive oil followed by the bacon. Cook until crisp.
9. Throw the bacon into the eggs, add the mayo, mustard, paprika, salt and pepper. Mix well.
10. Sprinkle with the green onion and serve.
11. Enjoy!

Saag Paneer

What do you get when you gently cook spinach and mustard leaves with a handful of warming spices, garlic and onion, then stir through paneer cheese? Heaven, that's what!

Cooks: 25 mins
Serves: 4
Net carbs: 6g
Fat: 5g
Protein: 15g

Ingredients:
- 1 Tbsp. butter or oil
- ¼ tsp. cumin seeds
- 2 green chili peppers, chopped
- 1" (2cm) ginger, chopped
- 10 cloves garlic, chopped
- 2 medium onions, chopped
- 1 bunch mustard leaves (can substitute with spinach)
- 1 bunch spinach
- ¼ cup (60ml) water
- 10 oz. (280g) paneer or cottage cheese, cut into small pieces
- 1 tsp. xanthan gum
- ½ tsp. turmeric
- ½ tsp. chili powder (or to taste)
- 2 tsp. ground coriander
- 1 tsp. salt

Method:
1. Open up your Instant pot, turn onto sauté and add the butter or oil.
2. Add the chili, ginger, garlic and onions. Cook for 5 minutes.
3. Next add the dried spices and cook for 30 seconds until fragrant.
4. Stir through the mustard greens, spinach and water.
5. Cover and cook on manual high pressure for 4 minutes.
6. Do a natural pressure release for five minutes then quick release the rest.
7. Open the pot and use an immersion blender to blend until smooth.
8. Sprinkle over the xanthan gum if you need to thicken it more. (I often don't bother.)
9. Switch onto sauté, add the paneer and cook for five minutes.
10. Serve and enjoy!

Cauliflower Mashed Potatoes

Everyone has their favorite cauliflower mash recipe, and this is mind. Perfect for your Instant pot and bursting with flavor, you'll wonder why you didn't think of adding garlic before.

Cooks: 10 minutes
Serves: 4
Net Carbs: 7g
Fat: 11g
Protein: 11g

Ingredients:
- 1 large head cauliflower cored and cut into large chunks
- 1 cup (235ml) water
- 1 Tbsp. butter
- 1/8 tsp. salt
- 1/8 tsp. pepper
- ¼ tsp. garlic powder
- 1 handful chives optional

Method:
1. Open your Instant pot, add the water, drop in the trivet and add the cauliflower.
2. Cover and cook on manual high pressure for 5 minutes.
3. Do a quick pressure release and open the lid.
4. Remove the cauliflower, pour away the water and return the cauliflower to the Instant pot.
5. Add the remaining ingredients and blend until you have a delicious puree.
6. Serve and enjoy!

Side Recipes

Cauliflower and Cheese

If you could be here now, you'd see me doing a silly dance in excitement THAT'S how much I love cauliflower cheese. Simple. Perfect. Everything you need.

Cooks: 20 minutes
Serves: 2
Net carbs: 7g
Fat: 21g
Protein: 11g

Ingredients:
- 2 cups (600g) cauliflower, chopped finely into 'rice'
- 2 Tbsp. cream cheese
- ½ cup (120ml) half and half
- ½ cup (60g) shredded sharp cheddar cheese
- ½ tsp. salt
- ½ tsp. pepper
- 1 ½ cups (350ml) water

Method:
1. Take a large heatproof bowl (that will fit into your Instant Pot) and combine all the ingredients. Stir well and cover with foil.
2. Pour the water into the Instant pot and add the trivet.
3. Place your bowl into the Instant pot then cover.
4. Cook on manual high for 5 minutes.
5. Do a natural pressure release for 10 minutes.
6. Meanwhile, heat your broiler.
7. Place your heatproof bowl under the broiler and heat until the cheese is brown.
8. Serve and enjoy!

Prosciutto Wrapped Spinach and Artichoke Chicken Bundles

I've included these here as a side dish, but really you could eat them as a snack, as a main course or whenever you like. They're extra special and perfect for those dinners when you really want to impress. Jus' sayin'.

Cooks: 30 minutes
Serves: 4
Net carbs: 6g
Fat: 13g
Protein: 62g

Ingredients:
- 1 ½ cups (45g) baby spinach
- 2 Tbsp. + 1 cup (235ml) water
- 1 clove garlic, minced
- ¼ cup (35g) onions, chopped
- 1 cup (170g) canned artichoke hearts, drained
- 1 cup (75g) mushrooms, sliced
- ¼ cup (60ml) coconut milk, canned
- 1/8 tsp. sea salt
- 1/8 tsp. black pepper
- 2 lb. (900g) chicken breasts, boneless
- 8 individual Prosciutto, sliced

Method:
1. Grab a large bowl, add the spinach and the water then place into the microwave for 1 minute. Drain well.
2. Place this into a food processor, with the garlic, onions, artichokes and mushrooms. Pulse until chopped.
3. Add the coconut milk and seasoning and pulse again. Pop to one side.
4. Butterfly the chicken breast and open up. Pour until thin.
5. Spread some of the filling across each, leaving space at the edges.
6. Roll up with the prosciutto and hold closed with toothpicks.
7. Now place the cup of water into the Instant pot and add the chicken.
8. Cover and cook on manual high pressure for 8 minutes.
9. Do a natural pressure release.
10. Serve and enjoy!

Yakisoba Noodles

Who wants to wait around all day for a snack or a side dish when you could have something yummy ready in less than half an hour?? Not me! This one is fast, simple but very tasty.

Cooks: 20 minutes
Serves: 4-6
Net carbs: 7g
Fat: 25g
Protein: 3g

Ingredients:
- 1 medium spaghetti squash
- 4 Tbsp. soy sauce
- 1 bag coleslaw mix (can sub with cabbage if required)
- 1 cup (75g) mushrooms, sliced (can leave out if wanted)
- 1 cup (235g) cooked chicken, shredded
- Green onion to garnish

Method:
1. Place the squash into the bottom of your Instant pot, add the water and cover.
2. Cook on manual high pressure for 8 minutes.
3. Do a quick pressure release and remove the squash. Place onto a chopping board.
4. Cut the squash in half and scoop out the seeds, then shred.
5. Pour the water out of the Instant pot and place the squash back inside.
6. Add the soy sauce, meat and coleslaw mix. Mix well.
7. Cover, turn onto sauté mode and cook for five minutes.
8. Sprinkle with green onion, serve and enjoy!

Low Carb Ham and Greens

Still missing your beans and greens? Don't worry- this ham and greens recipe will soon satisfy your cravings. Ready in just 20 minutes, it's the perfect side dish for any meal!

Cooks: 20 mins
Serves: 4
Net carbs: 6g
Fat: 12g
Protein: 4g

Ingredients:
- 6-8 cups (600-800g) collard greens, torn into pieces
- 1 large onion, chopped
- 6 cloves garlic
- 2 cups (150g) cooked ham, chopped
- 1 tsp. salt
- 1 tsp. pepper
- ¼ cups (60ml) water or stock
- 1 tsp. red pepper flakes
- 2 bay leaves
- 1 tsp. dried thyme

To serve....
- 1 Tbsp. Apple Cider Vinegar
- 1 tsp. Louisiana Hot Sauce or other vinegar-based hot sauce
- 1 tsp. liquid smoke

Method:
1. Place all ingredients into your Instant pot and stir well to combine.
2. Cover and cook on manual high pressure for 4 minutes.
3. Do a natural pressure release for five minutes.
4. Open, add the vinegar, liquid smoke and hot sauce. Stir well.
5. Serve and enjoy!

Baked Chicken Poppers

Love those easy 'throw-everything-into-a-pot-and-cook' kind of dishes, don't you? This one is cheesy, bacony and an awesome addition to your lazy weekends.

Cooks: 40 mins
Serves: 6
Net carbs: 3g
Fat: 14g
Protein: 7g

Ingredients:

- 1 lb. (450g) skinless chicken thighs, diced
- 1 ½ cups (260g) sweet peppers, diced
- 4 jalapeños, chopped (adjust to desired spice level)
- 2 oz. (45g) cream cheese
- 1 cup (125g) shredded cheese
- 2 tsp. chili powder
- ½ tsp. garlic salt
- ½ tsp. salt
- 4 slices bacon
- ¼ cup (40g) chopped scallions

Method:

1. Grease your Instant pot pan.
2. Take a bowl and combine everything except the bacon and scallions. Stir well.
3. Pour into the pan, cover with the bacon.
4. Cover and cook on manual high pressure for 30 minutes.
5. Do a quick pressure release.
6. Sprinkle with the scallions and bacon, then serve and enjoy!

Keto Brussel Sprouts

I'd always HATED Brussels with a passion. I mean, who doesn't? But once I'd tried these simple buttery sprouts, I was hooked.

Cooks: 10 minutes
Serves: 6
Net carbs: 6g
Fat: 0g
Protein: 3g

Ingredients:
- 1 lb. (450g) Brussels Sprouts
- ½ tsp. butter
- ¼ cup (60ml) water
- Pinch bacon bits
- Salt and pepper, to taste

Method:
1. Soak your Brussels Sprouts in water for five minutes.
2. Open your Instant pot and add the butter, water, bacon and seasonings.
3. Drain the sprouts and add to the Instant pot. Stir well.
4. Cover and cook on high for 4 minutes.
5. Do a quick pressure release.
6. Serve and enjoy!

Final Words

Now you have all the tools you need to stick to your Ketogenic diet, save loads of time, eat delicious and nourishing foods and watch those excess pounds fall off!

You *don't* have to keep looking into the mirror and wishing that you could somehow change the way you look, whilst feeling powerless to do so. You *don't* have to continue to feel ashamed of your body, wish that you had more energy or even wish that life wasn't so busy and you could actually find time to cook healthy food for a change.

Because you can! The answers are right here in this Instant Pot recipe book.

So, get yourself an Instant Pot right now, choose your favorite recipe from this book and get cooking! No excuses!

Thank You

I just wanted to quickly say thank you for reading this eBook. As you can imagine, testing over 100 recipes certainly isn't fast, but it certainly has been a whole lot of fun! There's nothing I love more in this world than sharing more fab recipes with my tribe- the people who care about their bodies and want to make a difference to their lives- YOU!

If you have a free moment or two, I'd really appreciate it if you could leave me a review on Amazon. This is what helps me to keep writing awesome recipe books like these.

I hope you really enjoy the recipes I've included and add them to your Keto 'go-to' list.

Made in the USA
Middletown, DE
03 November 2018

Keto Diet Instant Pot Cookbook

Delicious, Simple, and Easy Ketogenic Instant Pot Recipes for Smart People